CONTEMPORARY CREATIVE —— —— SPACES FOR —— CHILDREN ——

images
Publishing

Contents

Introduction

Written by Joey Ho
Design Partner,
P A L Design Group

Joey Ho is a design partner of P A L Design Group and has received over 180 awards and accolades, including the Andrew Martin International Interior Designer of the Year Award, FX International Design Award (United Kingdom), Interior Design Best of Year Award (United States), Frame Interior Award (Netherlands), IFI Global Award, and INSIDE World Festival of Interiors Award.

When discussing the program for children's spaces with clients, I usually take on the role of a spokesperson for children, to remind myself to change my adult mindset to perceive things as a child would. Working on spaces for children has been as gratifying as it has been joyful. It has also brought about a shift in my career, awakening my potential and my purity of heart.

When designing children's spaces, my starting point is to usually use the space to help kids master a new pace of life within a new a dimension, so as to discover infinite possibilities as they unleash their creativity toward day-to-day routine activities like washing hands or having meals.

It is a common misconception that children-related spaces need to be brightly colored. From what I have observed, while the impact of color does stimulate children's senses and even get them excited, an overuse of bright colors can also cause fatigue from over-stimulation and make it hard for children to concentrate. Thus, I prefer to choose from elements of nature to avoid an overly intense and strong visual language, but which still spark a type of "pure" joy in children's hearts while firing their imagination. I believe that the successful creation of children's spaces is not focused on fairytale arrangements, but in enabling adults and children to avoid the conscious and direct perception of a particular space as a "child's space," which usually occurs through highly conspicuous and blatant visual markers that denote the space to be a child' space. Children's spaces should ideally support a healthy lifestyle and incorporate room for creativity, so that children can have fun while learning new things.

The design of children's spaces should enable children to believe that growing up is a wonderful adventure and allow them to grow up in a space full of hope, expectation, and positivity. Therefore, I often endeavor to use nature's gifts to reflect vitality in a space's vibe and imbue the space with the power to support children's growth, as well as to fill children with excitement and encourage them to embrace growing up.

It is essential, as adults, that we put aside our adult outlooks and predispositions, and not be obsessed with molding children into what we think they should be. When designing spaces for children, it is important to remind ourselves that a child's development is a natural process and adults should not erase children's childhood and act only on their own experience; we should consider how we can help children build their own perception of the world.

We were children once, but gradually, we lost that childlike innocence. In conceptualizing a design, it helps to lay aside the aspects and elements of life that adults find appealing and open up to a child's world to seek inspiration in the happy moments of being a child and playing with other children—like how a simple game of hide-and-seek can make a child shriek with delight—in order to conceive how to incorporate heart-healing and elements that relate to children into the design. Being able to watch and enjoy how children respond with sincerity and intuition is the real meaning of my design, and I am both thankful and happy that I can again find my childlike innocence and curiosity and derive such happiness and contentment from designing children's spaces.

Play is important in a child's existence and its value goes far beyond our perception. Designing for children gives me the opportunity to look for imaginative ideas, strengthen my sense of humor, to dare to experience more, and overall, to learn to look at life from a child's point of view. It is a chance to leave behind the inevitable excessive worries and fears of the adult life in the adult world and re-examine each day to fill it with laughter, curiosity, and inquisitiveness, and once again find the innocence that we all once embraced.

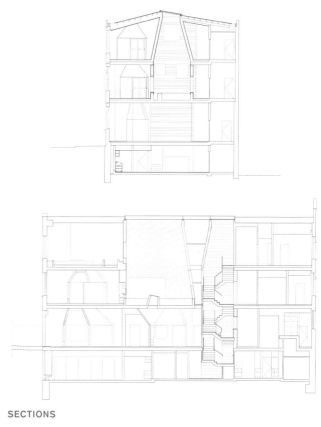

SECTIONS

DEVELOPMENTAL
SPACE

EAST SYDNEY EARLY LEARNING CENTRE

LOCATION:
DARLINGHURST, SYDNEY,
AUSTRALIA

COMPLETION: 2016

DESIGN: ANDREW BURGES
ARCHITECTS

PHOTOGRAPHY:
PETER BENNETTS

The East Sydney Early Learning Centre is an adaptive reuse of an existing four-level 1920s industrial building. The original structure was redesigned to house a childcare center and a community space in the dense neighborhood of Darlinghurst, Sydney, Australia.

The initial project brief suggested the closure of Berwick Lane next to the building to connect the John Birt Memorial playground with the existing building, so that the childcare center could occupy the lower three levels and the community center could be located on the top level. However, following a detailed urban analysis, community consultation, and a review by the City of Sydney, a far more imaginative solution was decided: the laneway would remain open and be significantly improved through a new stair construction, and the community center would be located at the lower ground level to animate and enliven the laneway, and the top three levels of the building would house the childcare, with a tree-house bridge link that crosses the laneway to lead to the ground level of the John Birt Memorial playground.

This fun and imaginative concept completely stripped the existing building—interiors, structure, and windows—to create a new four-story childcare and community building, and integrated the adjacent John Birt Memorial playground with the building through the tree-house bridge link. Works also included a refurbishment of the public domain, including Berwick Lane, and the streetscape.

THIRD-FLOOR PLAN

1 Community space
2 Community kitchenette
3 Staff room
4 Fire stairs
5 Kitchen and pantry
6 Services room
7 Entrance
8 Administration office
9 Main stairs
10 Playroom 2-3
11 Playroom 3-5
12 Veranda
13 Playroom 0-2
14 Outdoor play space
15 Coatroom
16 Courtyard
17 Bridge
18 Upper-playground platform
19 Lower playground
20 Raised deck

SECOND-FLOOR PLAN

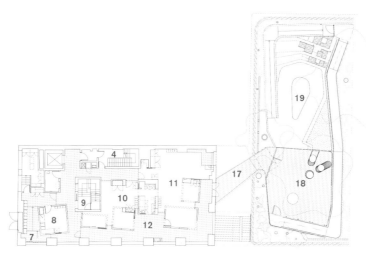

FIRST-FLOOR PLAN

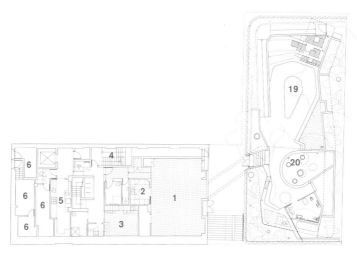

LOWER-GROUND-FLOOR PLAN

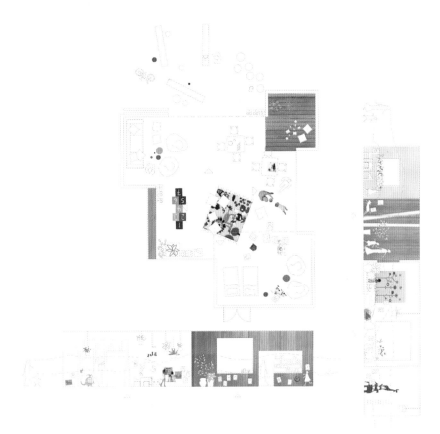

INTERNAL PLAY SPACE DIAGRAM

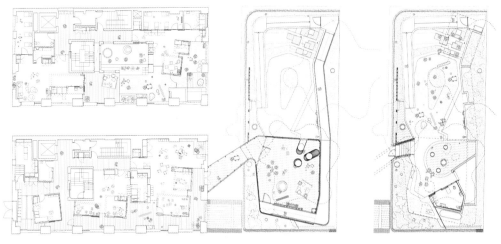

INTERNAL PROGRAM DIAGRAM

Against a backdrop of regulations and orthodoxies that focus on safe sightlines and transparency of structures—often leading to internal play spaces of wall-to-ceiling glazing—the philosophy of this project employs childhood imagination and play as its guiding framework and inspiration. The building has been conceived as a "mini-city," to enable experiential learning by reimagining the urban fabric at a child's scale. A series of playhouses or "pods" are connected by a network of social laneways and indoor parks, and a double-height centrally located lightwell over a large sandpit features the central area like an urban plaza. A rooftop garden connects the imaginative city of the building with the real one viewed beyond the building's boundaries.

The existing fabric is further animated with funnels of natural light that extend deep into the interior of the internal "pod" buildings, as well as the highly articulated interior, to tailor internal play spaces that create a range of spatial circumstances for the many learning activities, including active play, theatrical play, imaginative play, and quiet play.

Incorporating the tree-house bridge and ramp from the main building, the design of the John Birt Memorial playground focuses on creating a range of textural experiences and play forms as it organically unfolds around a jacaranda tree on the site to incorporate a mud pit, sandpit, amphitheater, outdoor classroom, and interactive water wall.

The center's features align with Sustainable Sydney 2030 city plan and include photovoltaic cells for rooftop solar capture; biofiltration at the window openings through internal planters and landscaping; mixed-mode ventilation and thermal zoning to contain and minimize areas that need air conditioning; alternative sources of user thermal comfort, including solar boosted hydronic heating and radiators; extensive use of lightwells to create daylighting deep into the internal fabric of the building; rainwater harvesting and use of water-efficient fixtures; green transportation planning that includes bicycle parking and staff changing facilities; sustainable materials, such as nontoxic materials with high recycled content and/or which are highly recyclable; low VOC finishes, and low formaldehyde furniture and products; and sustainable timber, and rapidly renewable and locally sourced materials.

All decisions on interior layout, material detailing, window openings, and finishes—including infrastructural elements such as fire sprinklers—were conceptualized to encourage a fascination with cities and city life, to serve as a guiding pedagogical tenet for the childcare.

DEVELOPMENTAL
SPACE

MAPLE STREET SCHOOL

LOCATION: BROOKLYN,
NEW YORK, UNITED STATES

COMPLETION: 2017

DESIGN: BAAO
ARCHITECTS, 4|MATIV
DESIGN STUDIO

PHOTOGRAPHY:
LESLEY UNRUH

Maple Street School, located in the rapidly changing neighborhood of Prospect Lefferts Gardens in Brooklyn was looking to expand into a second location; an upcoming mixed-use development had just the site. BAAO Architects and 4|MATIV Design Studio collaborated on this project to provide the cooperative school with a design program that would fit their spatial, as well as curricular needs, focusing on open and flexible spaces that integrate elements that would promote the school's educational philosophy.

The preschool presents itself as an extension of home—where cooperation and involvement are emphasized; where each child is nurtured in a warm and caring atmosphere; and where curiosity and play are central to learning. These concepts

shaped the design process and its outcome, with the designers selecting highly functional solutions to meet their needs.

The core of the floor plan lies within four interconnected main areas: a multipurpose room and three classrooms. The school's "cafe time" practice—daily group gatherings centered on snacks and promoting healthy eating habits and social engagement—inspired the inclusion of a central, semi-open kitchen located in the multipurpose room. The flexible kitchen design has open and closed states and was conceived with a variety of backdrops and graphics to cater to different kinds of staging scenarios and themes, such as a fun and engaging food truck setting.

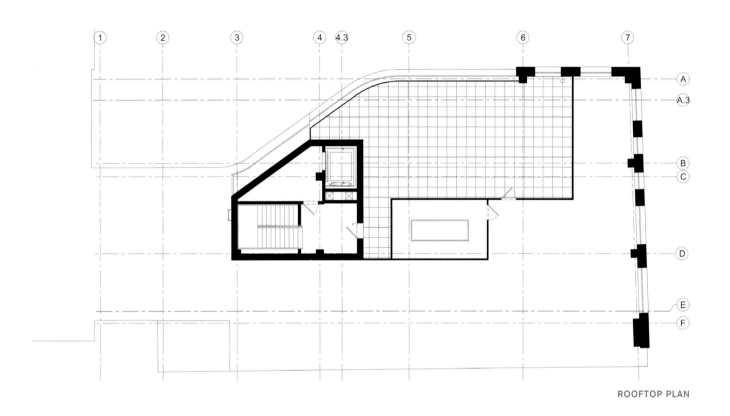

ROOFTOP PLAN

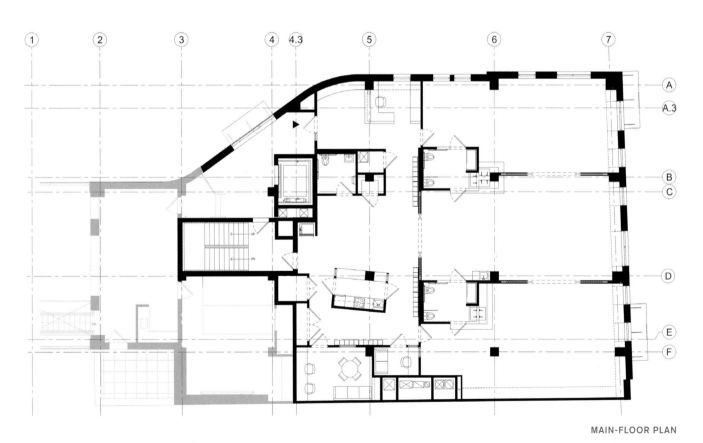

MAIN-FLOOR PLAN

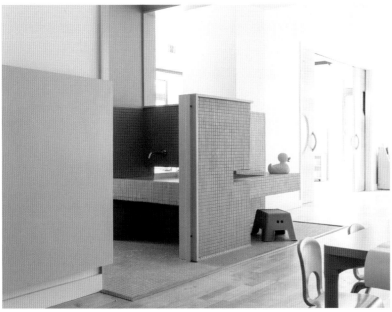

The classrooms are connected through large pairs of pocket doors with playful openings, allowing interaction between classrooms, and among children and staff. These large doors also provide flexibility for larger school events. Shared semi-open bathrooms are treated as focal points and also function as connecting elements, while providing the required visibility for staff members to keep an eye on the kids. Large trough-like play sinks run between classrooms and bathrooms, and become a key feature in promoting learning through water play and interaction.

The palette is warm and light, with maple wood and white walls that mark all spaces. This simplicity in interior aesthetics allows surfaces to act as backdrops for the children's handmade artworks, which is contrasted with accents of color from the pastel-toned tiles of the bathrooms and the bright-colored trims on the pocket door openings. The range of visual accents also stations a maple peg wall at the school's entry area. The fun and colorful pegs cheerfully greet children with a captivating burst of colors as they step into school, in a way also easing the daily change in environment from home to school.

Extending the use of colors in the design concept, an outdoor recreation area on the building's rooftop features a colorful rubber tile pattern with a large pixelated graphic of islands. The space is framed by a combination of warm cedar fencing and a patchwork of perforated aluminum screening. There are plans to set up a play structure and an outdoor classroom with a green wall in this space to expose children to nature and plants, while incorporating a space where they can play outdoors.

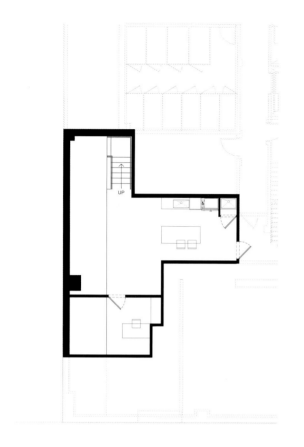

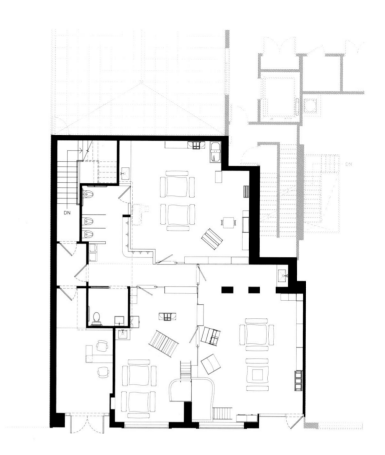

PLANS

DEVELOPMENTAL
SPACE

MI CASITA PRESCHOOL AND CULTURAL CENTER

LOCATION: BROOKLYN,
NEW YORK, UNITED STATES

COMPLETION: 2019

DESIGN: BAAO
ARCHITECTS, 4|MATIV
DESIGN STUDIO

PHOTOGRAPHY:
LESLEY UNRUH

This mix-use children's space, designed collaboratively by Barker Associates Architecture Office (BAAO Architects) and 4|Mativ Design Studio, is located in a new development in Brooklyn.

The school's program decides on three classrooms that occupy a large space with a wide ceiling span (equivalent to fifteen rooms) on the ground floor of the building, as well as a lower level for support

programing. The space is organized around an L-shaped trough sink that is transformed into a socialization and gathering area, and which, incidentally, also functions as a bathroom sink. Furniture is used to divide rooms to provide flexibility, so that the space can be tailored to accommodate a variety of functions, such as a venue for special events, such as performances organized by the school's artist-in-residence.

The school's focus on being a "home away from home," as well as encouraging children to learn from the different cultures that coexist in the melting pot of Brooklyn led the design team to incorporate graphic elements relating to home and city in the design of the space. A large house-shaped vitrine on the mezzanine will showcase seasonal displays that relate to the curriculum. Extending on the core concept of a home, house-shaped cutouts in the walls trail passages through the space and lead to delightful reading nooks tucked away like secret "caves."

Complementing the primary color palette of white, orange, and teal, mosaic murals in shades of pale blue arrange graphic iterations of a city skyline in the bathroom and trough sink area, adding interesting visual scenes that also anchor those areas. Color is used for dramatic effect throughout the whole space. Turquoise on the ceiling and light globes give the sense of being under a bright blue sky, while orange is used in cutouts in the walls and accent elements in the space, and also lines the stairs that lead down to the parent coworking space.

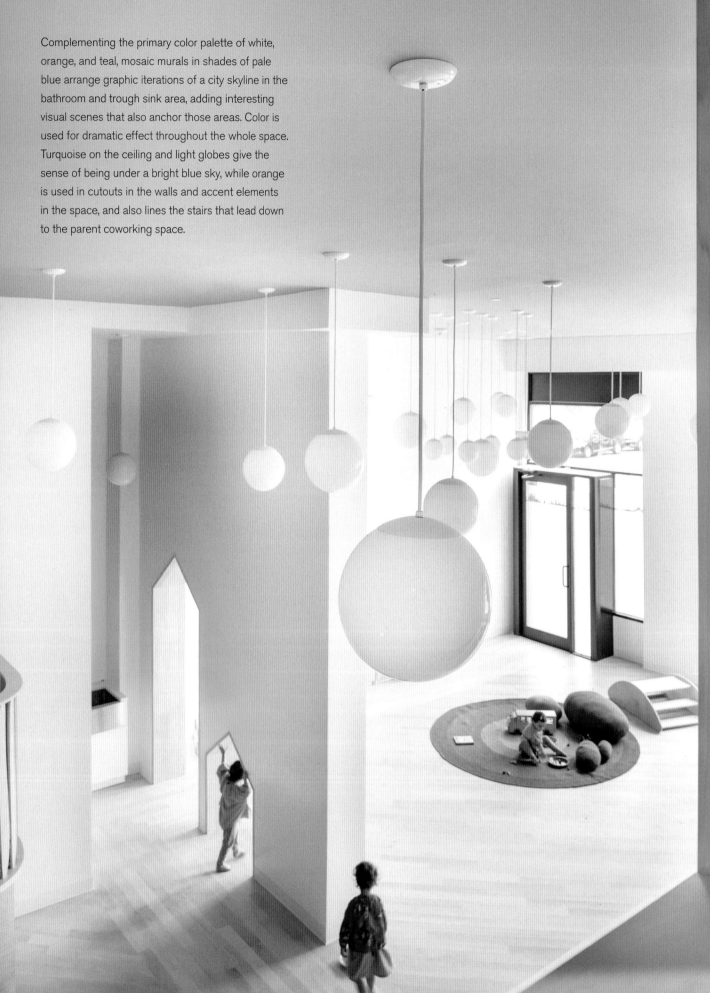

COMMUNITY LEARNING CENTER BEIJING

LOCATION: BEIJING, CHINA

COMPLETION: 2019

DESIGN:
HIBINOSEKKEI+YOUJI NO
SHIRO

PHOTOGRAPHY:
HIBINOSEKKEI+YOUJI NO
SHIRO

This childcare and learning center located amidst high-rise apartments in one of central Beijing's more posh neighborhoods targets a clientele of young local families. Rather than being a facility that strictly serves only children, it is also open to parents and the surrounding community.

The allotted space for the center is located on the ground floor of an existing half ellipse-shaped building that has a floor height of 13.1 feet (4 meters). "Street play in the city" as a key concept imparts the ambiance of Beijing's old city streets in the interiors.

In order to accommodate several activities at the same time, to fulfill the different needs and likes of the children, the big volume is distributed by placing container modules in an organic fashion. The containers are designed to be open to make it easy for children to recognize the function of each module's space. Such a design allows for easy expansion and contraction of the space and the activities within, simply by installing or removing modules according to the requirement of the facility and the education program.

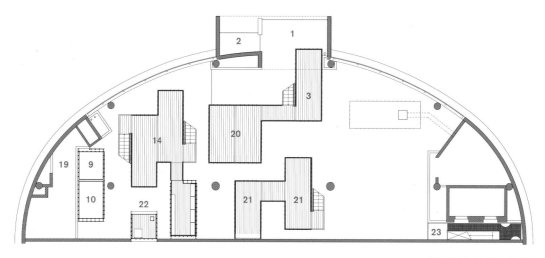

SECOND-FLOOR PLAN

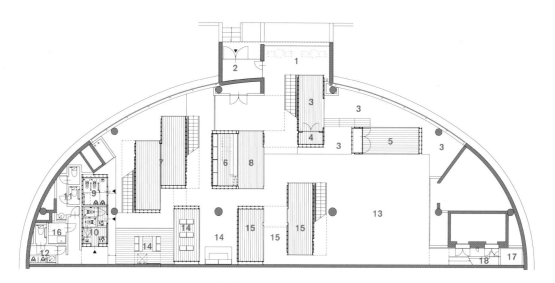

FIRST-FLOOR PLAN

1	Lounge and café	**9**	Restroom (0 to 4 years old)	**17**	Den
2	Entrance	**10**	Restroom (4 to 6 years old)	**18**	Storage
3	Community garden	**11**	Female restroom	**19**	Duct/vent space
4	Storage	**12**	Male restroom	**20**	Library and café
5	Kitchen	**13**	Indoor movement area	**21**	Multipurpose learning area
6	Office	**14**	Children's library	**22**	Toy library
7	Pre-kindergarten room	**15**	Workshop	**23**	Loft
8	Reception and shop	**16**	Nursing room		

The containers resemble the buildings along Beijing's streets and the aisles in between resemble the streets. The intimate scale of aisles adds a private element in this otherwise open space; its enclosing coziness is also favored by children and they can also use this area for such activities requiring concentration.

Adding handrails on the upper side of the containers creates terraced loft spaces, making the overall volume more dynamic and suitable for learning and playing. The design of the module is minimalistic, reflecting only two colors—charcoal gray on the exterior wall and the warm tones of wood on the floor, wall, and ceiling inside.

The added benefit of module architecture is the easy and swift supply of materials, as well as the convenient implementation and maintenance of the design.

1 Classroom
2 Communications room
3 Reception
4 Meeting room
5 Restroom
6 Kitchenette
7 Staff room
8 Laundry
9 Kitchen
10 Nappy change/restroom
11 Sleeping room
12 Project room
13 Car-seat storage
14 Accessible restroom
15 Director's office
16 Parking lot

FIRST-FLOOR PLAN

DEVELOPMENTAL
SPACE

NEW SHOOTS CHILDREN'S CENTRE

LOCATION: KERIKERI, NEW ZEALAND

COMPLETION: 2020

DESIGN:
SMITH ARCHITECTS

PHOTOGRAPHY:
AMANDA AITKEN

The hospitable climate of Kerikeri designs this children's center as a reflection of the environment, where children can interact with the space, and each other, in a more natural way.

The building is split into four pavilions that are sheltered by a large soaring roof form which ties the pavilions together. The pavilions span a large area of 7534.7 square feet (700 square meters), with each pavilion housing varying age groups of children. This design allows for free movement in a sheltered, yet open and unconfined space.

The expansive roof shelters the pavilions, and much of the space around them, from sun and rain, providing all-weather spaces for a range of activities and functions, such as outdoor dining and external circulation, and intersperses access routes with pocket gardens throughout the design. The units are designed to face the striking Pohutakawa tree located in the heart of this purpose-built center, to encourage children to connect with the natural environment. While the architectural design reflects the local culture, the blurring on indoor boundaries inspires open-ended exploration and discovery throughout the center.

A natural material palette creates a warm and welcoming space for children in the center; it features horizontal timber cladding styled with aluminum joinery to create a lighter and more natural environment. Large sliding doors in the pavilions maximize the connection to the outdoor playground and allow an abundance of natural daylight and ventilation to ensure optimum quality in the internal environment, so as to maintain the health and well-being of the children.

The interior of each classroom has been specifically designed by the New Shoots team to give children a unique learning environment, with features that cater for the unique needs of each age group. Custom designed cabinetry and furniture is implemented to ensure every space has been well-considered, creating a cohesive feel that carries through from the overall architecture and form of the building.

The luscious outdoor area takes full advantage of the winterless climate in north New Zealand and provides a nature-inspired playground for the *tamariki* (children) to explore and make discoveries to remember.

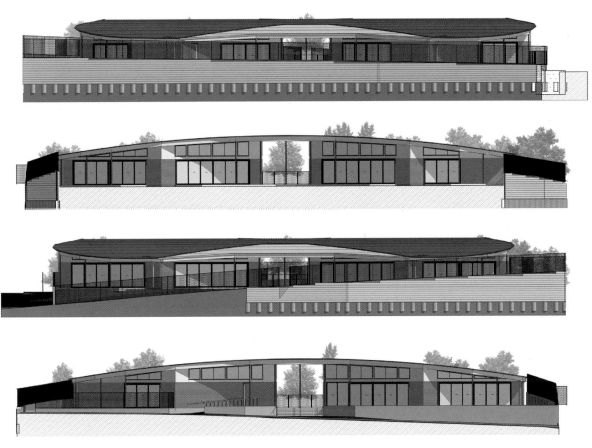

ELEVATIONS

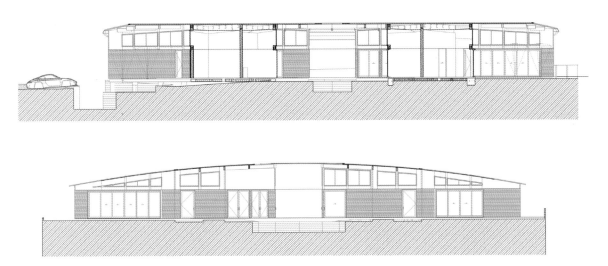

SECTIONS

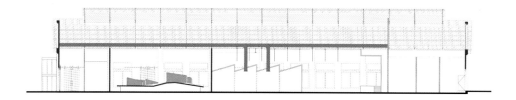

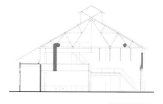

SECTIONS

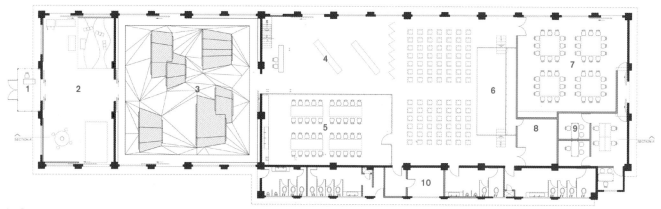

FLOOR PLAN

1   Reception
2   Introduction to arts and crafts
3   Library
4   Exposition center
5   Arts and crafts room
6   Theater
7   Adults' learning room
8   Warehouse
9   Offices
10 Open space

DEVELOPMENTAL
SPACE

NIÑOS CONARTE

LOCATION: MONTERREY,
MEXICO

COMPLETION: 2013

DESIGN: ANAGRAMA

PHOTOGRAPHY: CAROGA
FOTOGRAFO

Monterrey, the third largest city in Mexico, is best known for its beautiful mountains and strong industrial backbone. In the heart of the city is Fundidora Park, a unique specimen of industrial archaeology, which was previously a massive steelworks and foundry that was established in 1900. The park is home to extensive gardens, museums, convention centers, auditoriums, theme parks, and cultural bodies such as Conarte (Council for Culture and the Arts of Nuevo León).

Conarte sought to create a space for children in this park that would foster a love of reading and learning. The children's library and cultural center is situated inside a warehouse-like building, which is a heritage site of the state, and which cannot be reconstructed or adjusted in architecture. So, instead, the design cleverly enhances the building with a complementing and creative contemporary update that retains the original building structure and design.

The result is a multipurpose, asymmetrical reading platform that simulates Monterrey's mountainous topography. The bookshelves are not only used as storage, but also serve as a dynamic space where children can play and learn, and fire their imagination in a comfortable and inviting reading environment.

The installation's colorful and geometric aesthetic contrasts directly with its antique, industrial host, elevating both elements in a cheerful and unique way. The color palette of the design also makes the space projection more harmonious, so that it

is easier for children to settle down in the space and get engrossed in the pages of a book. The undulating design of the ground, shaped like a hillside, also increases the interest quotient of the space, and at the same time, provides a certain degree of privacy for the children. The carpet has also been specifically selected to improve the comfort level of the children when reading, overlooking no detail in the design of this library, so as to create a space where children can relax, read, and imagine along with the adventures and tales in the pages of books.

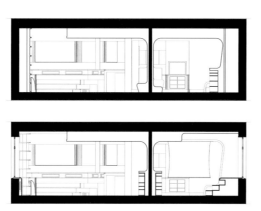
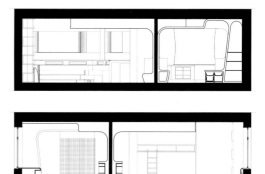

SECTIONS

DEVELOPMENTAL
SPACE

KIDS CLUB

LOCATION:
SAINT-PETERSBURG,
RUSSIA

COMPLETION: 2016

DESIGN:
ANDREY STRELCHENKO

PHOTOGRAPHY:
DMITRII TSYRENSHCHIKOV

Kids Club employs dedicated zones in its design to allow children a sense of independence as they move from one zone into the next, realizing their unique potential on their own terms. Open planning helps the child to feel free through the freedom to move around; activity zones set the stage for energetic pursuits; cozy nooks provide areas for rest and alone time; and workshops deliver a fun place to unleash creativity.

Each space features a different expression through a range of materials: concrete, ceramics, fabric, and even elements of nature, like trees. This variety also, respectively, permits different tactile perceptions within each zone to help children learn, understand the world around them, and explore different materials and surfaces through touch, as well as how they feel about them.

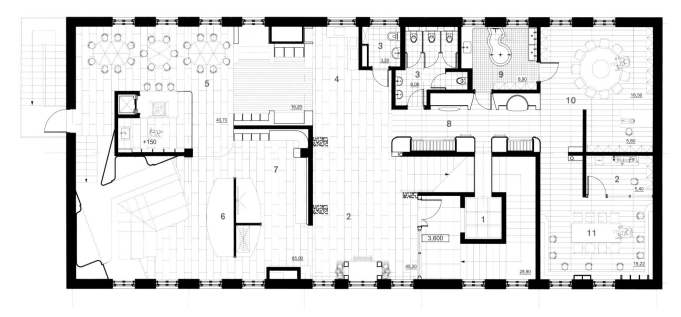

SECOND-FLOOR PLAN

1	Tree labyrinth	7	Media library
2	Rock-climbing wall	8	Private niches
3	Restrooms	9	Room of water
4	Montessori	10	Needlework workshop
5	Dining room	11	Workshop
6	Theater		

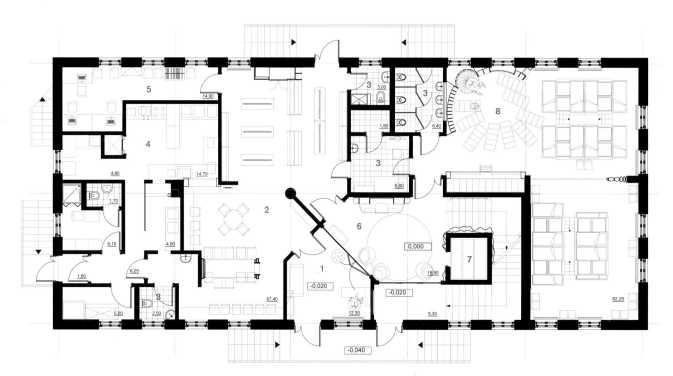

FIRST-FLOOR PLAN

1	Tambour space	5	Office
2	Hall	6	Corridor
3	Restrooms	7	Tree labyrinth
4	Kitchen	8	Room of the dream rest

The flow of water and its properties are also referenced through various forms and design implements that do not often marry in day-to-day living. These include curvilinear walls, the house-window, niches for games and napping, "caves," labyrinths, and sink reservoirs. These elements remove established typical perceptions of a child's surroundings and gives the young minds a chance at imagination and creativity.

The design of Kids Club is tailored around a few key points. The first is children's behavior. Time was taken to observe preschoolers in different activity, games, and venue scenarios to understand their needs, ways of interaction, and responses. Weather conditions of the area and how these would affect the activities of the children—in turn deciding how and where they would spend their time on the premises—were also considered.

Adding to these, the design also takes into account age and anthropometrical stats, so that every child feels comfortable and can exercise independence in carrying out tasks. Child safety also played a role and care was taken to protect children from dangerous encounters, such as electrical units and hazardous objects. This was ensured by adhering to the construction rules and sanitary standards set for institutions for children. Consultations with teachers at the initial stage of the project also helped shape the project and knot the loose ends.

The different age groups of children that the facility would serve offered a challenge, as well as the opportunity to be creative in the design. The solution was to regard the overall audience as one large family and provide a space where all areas are opened equally to everyone, with several

zones where children of different ages can play as equals. It was also essential that this space allows children the freedom to choose their activity and be engaged with a range of options. In creating an atmosphere in which children naturally develop a curiosity to investigate and explore the space, we help children look for answers to their questions, and successfully find them.

OLIOLI

LOCATION: DUBAI, UNITED
ARAB EMIRATES

COMPLETION: 2017

DESIGN: SNEHA DIVIAS
ATELIER

PHOTOGRAPHY: NIKOLA
AND TAMARA

In this project, the designers were tasked to create a space that reimagines antiquated playgrounds to provide children with a fun-filled, challenging, creative, stimulating, and enriching alternative to passive play, thereby nurturing their sense of curiosity in an exploratory setting. The result defines a conceptual journey through galleries. The project is whimsical and entices children's curiosity using vibrant color accents against neutral materials, and cleverly retains the existing architectural structure of the building. The passage through the arches displays a captivating rhythm of light and shadow, and textured materials such as concrete, wood, and metal add a sensory layer to the experience.

OliOli is a concept inspired from the conflation of four things: children's museums, innovative playgrounds, children's art museums/studios, and maker spaces or creative labs.

These elements iterate a purpose-built learning sanctuary for children, providing an opportunity for creative, open-ended, unstructured, and limitless play, while also creating a space where they are expected to spend two to three hours each visit.

SECOND-FLOOR PLAN

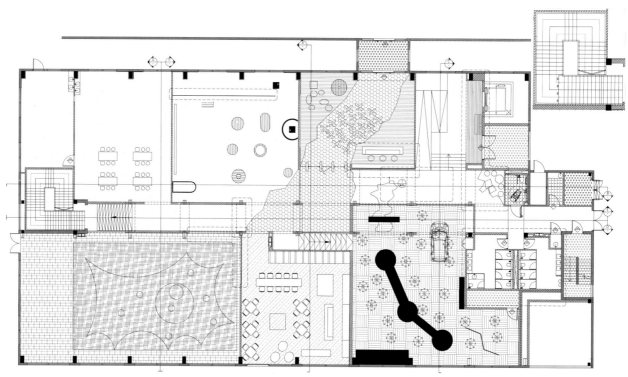

FIRST-FLOOR PLAN

In addition to common areas such as the reception, restrooms, corridors, café, birthday party rooms, and quiet spaces for kids, the facility features eight galleries spread across the floors. Abundant natural light in the space and an expansive environment allows for natural exploration rather than over-stimulation. Every corner is embellished with eye-catching details, from bird and butterfly motifs to pops of color and quirky sculptures; children discover something new and exciting each visit.

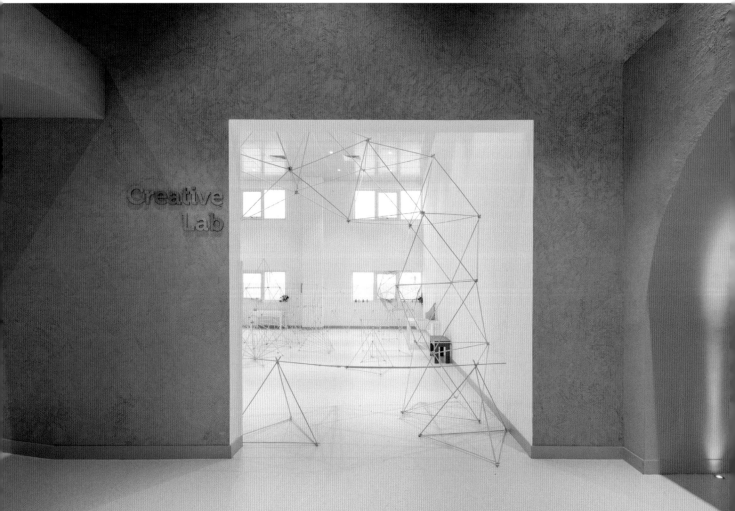

In total, the galleries present over forty interactive and whimsical activities for the children, unlocking their creativity at every turn to spark a genuine love of learning. A team of friendly staff offers encouragement to urge the children on to explore and discover in their own way, as how they like to—here, there is neither a right way, nor a wrong way. It is important that the children participate in a way that is comfortable to them, at their own pace, to inculcate a curious nature to learn and discover.

Each gallery has its own identity, but at the same time also follows the consistent, clean, and interesting design language that features neutral materials interspersed with OliOli's brand colors.

Designers ensured that each gallery had its own identity but at the same time followed the consistent uncluttered, clean, and interesting design language with neutral materials complemented with the branding colors.

DEVELOPMENTAL
SPACE

TRIVANDRUM INTERNATIONAL SCHOOL EARLY LEARNING CENTER

LOCATION: TRIVANDRUM, INDIA

COMPLETION: 2019

DESIGN: RANJIT JOHN ARCHITECTS AND EDUCATION DESIGN INTERNATIONAL

PHOTOGRAPHY: ANDRE J FANTHOME

TRINS Early Learning Center (TRINS) is a preschool with a vision toward adaptive elementary education. Human behavior and instincts are often influenced by spaces, and the design of one is a sensitive responsibility—more so in this project because kids and education are key aspects of a primary school.

The design intent of TRINS focuses on empowering education by creating spaces that fulfill emotional, physical, and social needs. The learning center is a four-story building with an area of 20,000 square feet (1,858.1 square meters) and can accommodate 200 children of diverse age groups, starting from six months up to six

years. The narrative for the spaces' interior design amalgamates comforting sights, sounds, and scents for the holistic development of the children; interiors are designed to provide toddlers and preschoolers with elements to explore and experiment with, and which help to expand little imaginations.

Each floor has seamlessly connected learning and activity spaces, both indoors and outdoors, within divisions named Caring Spaces and Learning Places. Services are also built into individual floors and include restrooms, teachers' collaborative areas, and administrative units. Each floor is also specific to the class level and the children's age group.

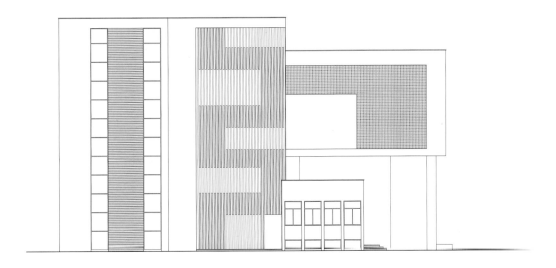

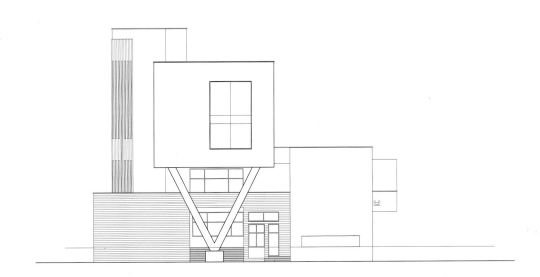

ELEVATIONS

SECOND-FLOOR PLAN

1 Landscaped terrace
2 Toddlers' zone
3 Staircase
4 Teachers' area
5 Restrooms
6 Courtyard cutout
7 Infants' sleeping area

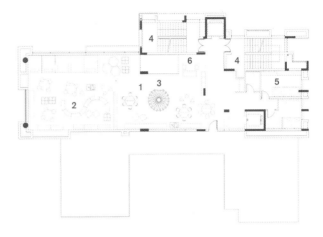

THIRD-FLOOR PLAN

1 Kindergarten-1
2 Kindergarten-2
3 Cozy "nests"
4 Staircase
5 Restroom
6 Teachers' area

BASEMENT PLAN

1 Childrens' kitchen
2 Staircase
3 Lift
4 Café
5 Staff changing room
6 Teachers' training area
7 Play area
8 Storeroom
9 Lounge

FIRST-FLOOR PLAN

1 Discovery zone
2 Kitchen
3 Staircase
4 Reception and discovery zone
5 Restroom
6 Waiting area
7 Meeting room
8 Center head (office)
9 Administration area
10 Pool

As one enters the building through the entrance foyer, they experience the grandeur of the space, courtesy of a double-volume reception that features a table that supports the backdrop. The reception houses a lounge, with seating, and a central discovery zone, complete with seating and storage spaces. The level also includes an administration space and an indoor and outdoor discovery zone that accentuates the playfulness of the space.

The first floor is dedicated to infants and toddlers. Keeping their requirements in mind, the floor houses an infant zone, toddler zone, feeding space, and a nap zone. All the spaces have soft flooring and wall padding—up to 4 inches (10 centimeters) high—so that kids can play freely and discover. The spaces are visually connected through either transparent glass or semi-transparent rafters. The physical safety of the children has also been carefully considered and to that end, there are no sharp corners or harmful materials incorporated in the design. An outdoor terrace with a sandpit keeps the young ones entertained with joyful play time.

The second floor of the building has learning spaces designed for the pre-kindergarten age group. With two classrooms and a combination of different types of seating, this multipurpose space is cheerful, safe, and can be adapted to different activities and functions. The furniture and storage spaces have been designed to the requirement of kids at the pre-kindergarten level. The classrooms have safety guards, multifunctional pods, and soft padding on the floors. A quiet zone outside the classroom serves as a welcome reprieve from the many activities and classes taking place in the institute, and the activity zone is a playful outdoor space that is dedicated to literary and performing arts. The terrace is designed with tensile sun shades for the comfort of the children; alongside this area, an easel has been set up, near the sandpit, planters, and a "mess-friendly" area where the children can play to their heart's content without there being concern of surfaces getting damaged.

The third and last floor has spaces made for the kindergarten level. Apart from a dedicated quiet/reading zone, the floor has two visually connected classrooms. As an extension to the whole design, the classrooms have cozy "nests," flexible furniture, storage, and seating. The monotony of a typical classroom typology is eagerly disrupted with a rock climbing wall, cutouts in the wall, and patterned soft flooring to create an interesting and exciting space for the children. As a complement, a quiet zone, supplementing as a reading nook, is created to support quiet reading time for the children to delve into the interesting world of books.

Complete with pods for various hands-on activities and play-based learning and storytelling, the spaces merge together functionally and aesthetically. Stepped seating and storage spaces, along with flexible furniture arrangements make the spaces versatile, add value to them, and make the learning journey impactful.

The design of the learning pods draws inspiration from the houseboats of Kerala to add some local context to the design. The outdoor spaces are provided with active play areas, water play areas, a sound garden, and kitchen garden, as well as includes areas for sensory and tactile activities. Thus, the entire design recapitulates a learning hub for infants, toddlers, and preschoolers, with elements to explore, discover the familiarity of home within, and build an environment that is as enriching as it is engaging.

M.Y.FROG: CREATIVE ACTIVITIES CENTER FOR CHILDREN

LOCATION: XANTHI,
GREECE

COMPLETION: 2020

DESIGN:
KYRIAKOS N. MICHAILIDIS /
MNK DESIGN STUDIO

PHOTOGRAPHY:
GRIGORIS LEONTIADIS
PHOTOGRAPHY

Located in the city of Xanthi, M.Y.frog is a certified creative activities center for children that aims to make the most of pastimes with fun and creative activities for children. Housed in a 1,076.4-square-foot (100-square-meter) space, it consists of two activity rooms, a teachers' room that also operates as a reception for parents and children who visit, and sanitary services adapted for children.

Children aged five to twelve are accommodated in specially designed activity areas to broaden their cognitive horizons, develop their skills and special talents, cultivate their character, and help them become independent and autonomous. By participating in various educational programs, children get to know the principles and values of teamwork and being in team, which is hoped will contribute to them becoming active members of the society in the future—hence, the center aims to help build stable foundations for their future.

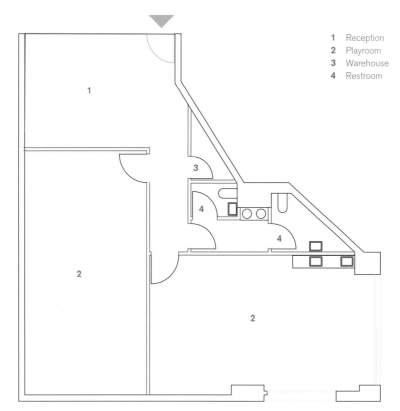

1 Reception
2 Playroom
3 Warehouse
4 Restroom

FLOOR PLAN

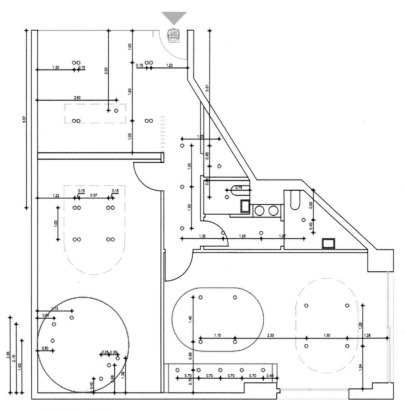

LIGHTING DESIGN

The spaces, designed with the above principles in mind, are based on children's imagination and their innate tendency to explore and respond. Two rooms are created with the potential to be transformed into a single one; this space is divided by a furniture unit that functions as a library, with an opening that facilitates the transition from one space to another. The main goal of the design is to encourage the development of children's aesthetic perception, not only through visual stimulation, but also through the dynamics of architectural elements.

Linear elements and curved shapes work harmoniously, with different colors characterizing the constructions in each room. This, combined with the naturalness and warmth of wood—used in the floor, wall, and ceiling—imparts a three-dimensional feeling of completeness to the spaces in the center.

ELEVATIONS

HOUSE OF WONDER, CAMBRIDGE

LOCATION: CAMBRIDGE, NEW ZEALAND

COMPLETION: 2020

DESIGN: SMITH ARCHITECTS

PHOTOGRAPHY: MARK SCOWEN

House of Wonder is sited near the hidden lakes of the beautiful Cambridge region in New Zealand. The early childcare learning center accommodates ninety children, from infants to age six, and provides a warm and inviting environment for Cambridge's *tamariki* (children) with state-of-the-art facilities, bright open-plan classrooms, and spacious outdoor play areas that enable children to explore and move freely.

Located in a countryside setting, the center has been designed as a series of "houses" connected through gardens and walkways to create a community-focused village. The arrangement of the classrooms are broken down into smaller barn-like forms that are planned around natural outdoor playscapes and covered

timber walkways. This design enables the center to accommodate to different age groups of children by encouraging them to identify their respective hub as a home base.

With a total built area of 6781.2 square feet (630 square meters), the building form is made up of a sequence of five traditional gable roofs. The fragmented nature of the building is woven together with external pathways; this creates a seamless indoor–outdoor flow.

To deliver a modern feel in the environment, vertical corrugate and timber cladding is used. This aesthetic is enhanced with nature, with tall pine trees planted throughout the spaces to provide a lush backdrop within the context of Cambridge.

The philosophy that shapes House of Wonder is the view that a child's environment is their third teacher. Along this belief, it was vital to create a connection to nature and the outdoor. Large sliding doors and covered timber canopies facilitate this flow between indoors and outdoors to seamlessly surround children with elements of nature. The large door openings also provide passive cooling and allow fresh air circulation within the interior, as well as the filtering in of natural daylight, reducing the need for artificial lighting.

Incorporating the Reggio Emilia Approach®—an educational philosophy that advocates that a child has "strong potentialities for development and (is) a subject with rights, who learns through the hundred languages belonging to all human beings, and grows in relations with others"—in its curriculum, the center also features specially designed art studios to accommodate smaller groups of children for creative play, such as expressing themselves creatively through art projects.

FIRST-FLOOR PLAN

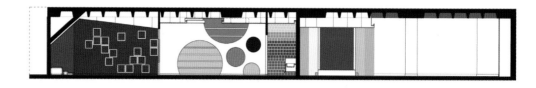

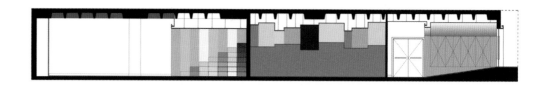

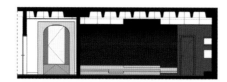 

SECTIONS

KALORIAS CHILDREN'S SPACE

LOCATION: OEIRAS, PORTUGAL

COMPLETION: 2013

DESIGN: ESTÚDIO AMATAM

PHOTOGRAPHY: ESTÚDIO AMATAM

"In reality we work with few colors. Which gives the illusion (that) their number is being put in its rightful place."

Pablo Picasso

Designing this space for children led to a journey through time and space, in search of that restlessness that exists in the background of all beings—the imagery that makes us dream, and which we always seek whenever we reach for our most childlike and creative essence. This refurbishment project was an opportunity to create a retreat for young people, where they could set free all their creativity. In order to achieve this, it was essential to use color to stimulate the spatial and visual perception, which led to the use of color psychology in this intervention.

The existing space was located within the Kalorias Health Club complex in Oeiras and was defined by two large rooms and a large hall, which had initially served corporate events. Stipulations in the brief suggested that the redesign would need to include: A multipurpose room that would be large

and versatile, and which would allow different uses— as a reading room dedicated to academic support and for watching films, reading books, and the educational use of computer equipment; a visual arts room that would support the main function of crafts and visual expression; and a playroom for the purpose of fun and physical games. Based on these programmatic needs, the spaces were adapted by retaining most of the existing structures, with the addition of new elements. Regardless of whether the logic of the new adaptations incorporated new forms, colors, textures or graphics, at the end of it, they needed to fulfill an important task: to reflect a symbolism that would allow anyone who entered the space to be transported to a dreamlike reality. This challenge guided the designers away from typical conceptualization processes and architectural guidelines, leading to the dematerialization of usual notions on spatial equilibrium, in order to arrive at a detachment from established practices and notions in reality. The result is a space that is created playful and with a distinct identity associated with children.

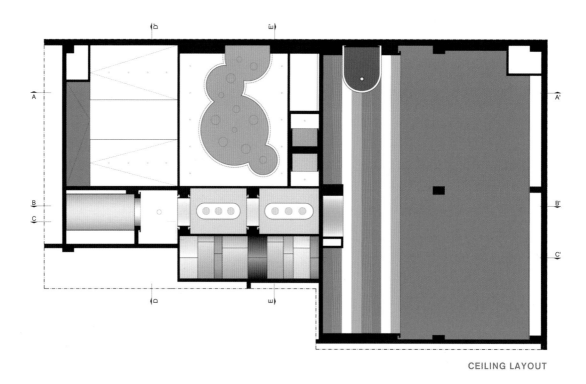

CEILING LAYOUT

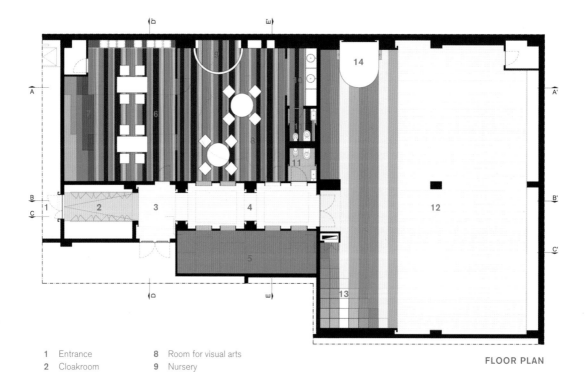

FLOOR PLAN

1	Entrance	**8**	Room for visual arts
2	Cloakroom	**9**	Nursery
3	Hall	**10**	Wet area
4	Gallery	**11**	Restroom
5	Playroom	**12**	Multipurpose room
6	Reading room	**13**	Colored Tetris-mountain
7	Amphitheater	**14**	Stage

With varying unique features, each room is a destination that narrates a special story. In all of them, there are new design elements that are combined with a surprise of colors, helping to contextualize the spaces in a very particular way.

The corridor is the unifying space that communicates with all rooms and ties together the spatial and formal language. The different arches—the main distinctive feature of the corridor—symbolize a passage, like a promenade for little princesses and small kings, and also serve as window displays for the different rooms/functions.

The reading room, which features a small amphitheater, allows children to draw and write around a huge blackboard that doubles as a huge screen for watching movies and cartoons. The room for visual arts prioritizes curves and organic shapes, and vibrant colors to stimulate visual expression. The huge blue ceiling that sparkles with white lamps is reminiscent of a starry sky, while the pierced walls uncover small hiding spaces and create unique visual effects.

In the playroom, the green carpet dilutes the ground into the wall, which is wrapped in a set of colored slopes deconstructing the ceiling. The last room at the end of this magical corridor functions as the most versatile space and is defined as an open area and a playful space that is distinguished by its colored Tetris-mountain and a small stage for theatrical performances.

Observing the different ways that children adapt and appropriate the space as their own speaks for the success of this new space that has been reborn with lively colors, unusual shapes, and unique features, and which aspires to help children discover and unlock their best potential.

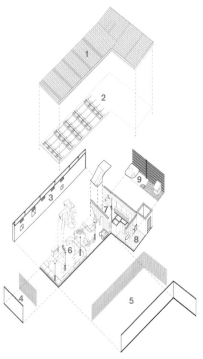

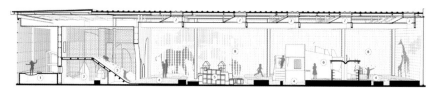

EXPLODED AXONOMETRIC DIAGRAM

1 Roof with skylights
2 Ceiling with skylights
3 North façade
4 West glass façade and pixelated screen
5 South glass façade and pixelated screen
6 Main play area
7 Transition hall
8 Entrance hall
9 Outdoor play area

SECTION

PLAYVILLE

LOCATION: BANGKOK, THAILAND

COMPLETION: 2018

DESIGN: NITAPROW

PHOTOGRAPHY: KETSIREE WONGWAN

One of the most fundamental methods in helping children to fully explore their physical and cognitive abilities is movement. Playville conceives multiple architectural terrains and topographical structures as a tool to encourage children to move in countless ways through a creative concept that employs nature's geological diversity as a guide in its execution. Five programmatic zones that are iterated in nature-inspired themes see the concept through.

The Entrance (Fog and Tree Tunnel)
Gradient film, a wood-covered floor, walls, lockers, and archways come together to suggest a solid, warm, and enchanting entrance. Hardwood flooring shifts to low-impact flooring as the area moves into more active spaces, to accommodate little ones that start to explore and run about as they get charged with excitement.

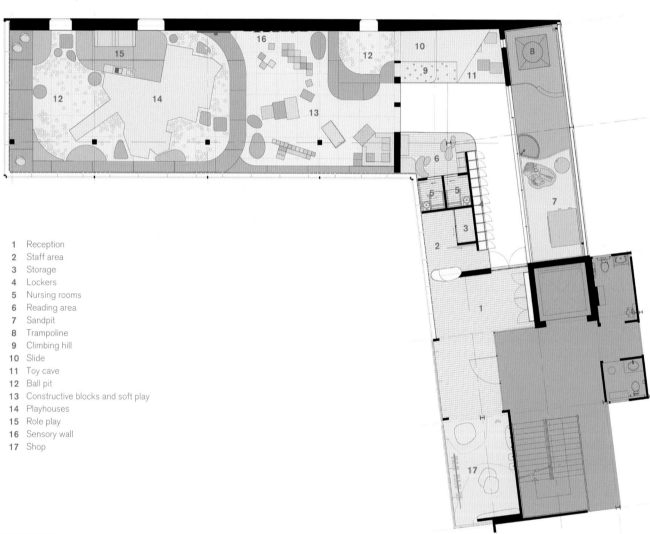

1   Reception
2   Staff area
3   Storage
4   Lockers
5   Nursing rooms
6   Reading area
7   Sandpit
8   Trampoline
9   Climbing hill
10 Slide
11 Toy cave
12 Ball pit
13 Constructive blocks and soft play
14 Playhouses
15 Role play
16 Sensory wall
17 Shop

FLOOR PLAN

The Retail (Cliff and Boulders)

An interchangeable wall shelving system is placed along the main terrazo wall. Pebble-like counters encourage a smooth circulation loop and a visual continuity between the central display cluster and the front display unit. A large mirror wall sets up a seemingly generous display corner with a multicolor shelving display unit at the back corner of the store.

The Transition (Hill and Burrow)

A wooden raised platform creates both an elevated terrain for climbing and sliding, while incorporating an intimate hideaway beneath it. The elevated terrain is physically connected to the main play area at one end and visually connected to the covered outdoor area at the other.

The Covered Outdoor (Dune and Oasis)

Specifically placed along the cooler east-facing façade, the sandpit invites the exuberant dives of little feet excited to explore and play. If soaring in the air is more their style, children can bounce away and take to the air like weightless balloons on the grass-covered trampoline.

The Main Play Area (Island and Lakes)

Pieces of custom foam block are put together to form a ball pit in the main play area. Continuous circulation loops have been specifically created around the playhouse and the island to support little children's natural behavior of seeking repetition.

Multiple skylight planes installed throughout the area bring natural light into the space to create a well-lit, cheerful ambiance. As most of the exterior walls face the strong southern and western sunlight, a large glass façade, together with a system of floor-to-ceiling pixelated felt screen was chosen to maintain the visual connection between the interior and the exterior, while ensuring the reduction of solar heat gain. This outfit also enhances the acoustic performance of the playground.

Each pixel strand in the screen begins with a square pixel at the top and incrementally transforms into a circle over twenty-one variations, thereby increasing light aperture as the screen reaches the ground. These units are loosely threaded with a vertical sling, allowing them to be receptive to physical touch. This enables the screen to "project" throughout the day, creating light and shadow displays similar to those found in nature.

The pixels are also printed with images of wild animals and natural landscapes, such that the image comes into view and forms the full picture when the individual pixels are in the correct alignment. The scale and the subtlety of the entire screen challenges the viewer's perception, such that they may have to take a step back and be at the correct distance, and aligned with the right perspective, as only then will the full picture and the real story reveal itself.

FAMILY BOX QINGDAO

LOCATION: QINGDAO,
SHANDONG PROVINCE,
CHINA

COMPLETION: 2015

DESIGN:
CROSSBOUNDARIES

PHOTOGRAPHY: XIA ZHI

The rapid progress of early childhood education in China led to Family Box opening its sixth branch in Qingdao, China. The two-floor 47,361-square-foot (4,400-square-meter) facility offers the establishment's usual suite of services, which includes a children's swimming pool, classrooms, open play areas, and a café. Occupying a generous corner space within a shopping mall, the center introduces its facility with a transition zone that holds a library, retail functions, and trial class space for potential customers interested in its services; this space also directs members to the pool and members-only zones.

Creative Spatial Solutions for a Compact Program

As children and their guardians enter, a consciously selected limited interior palette conscientiously filters out the external stimuli in the shopping mall. Yellow, blue, and green are selected as the main design colors to represent the city of Qingdao, and each color is associated with a special design feature to make the corresponding interior function division more recognizable for children. The floors and stairs are designed in yellow, while multifunctional smart spaces are presented in blue.

FIFTH-FLOOR PLAN

1 Lobby/public area
2 Shop
3 Library
4 Reception/coat and shoe storage
5 Open class and playtime area
6 Storytelling area
7 Small multifunctional hall
8 Soft play area
9 Mechanical room
10 Restroom/rest area
11 Play frame
12 Pool lobby
13 Pool corridor
14 Male changing room
15 Family changing room
16 Female changing room
17 Coach's room
18 Pool
19 Pool storage
20 Large multifunctional hall
21 Café
22 Art play area
23 First-aid room
24 Dance classroom
25 Open multifunctional classroom
26 Music classroom
27 Musical play area
28 Art and handcraft classroom
29 Sensory play area
30 Nap area/baby room/VIP room
31 Sand and water play area
32 Science classroom
33 VIP room
34 Corridor
35 Picnic/lounge area
36 Mini market
37 Cooking classroom

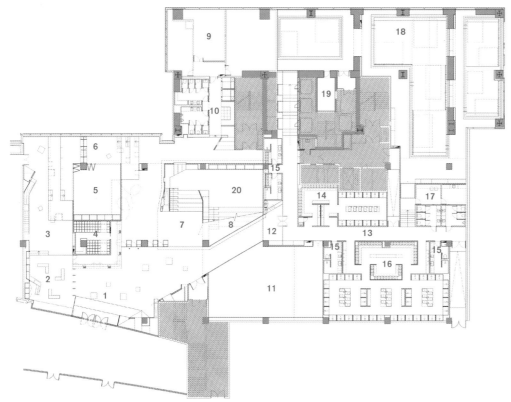

FOURTH-FLOOR PLAN

Conventional walls are transformed into green cutout smart volumes to incorporate more areas in the program—as requested by Family Box—so as to maximize the available space.

When closed, rooms and play areas function independently to accommodate classes and group activities, however, clever movable walls open up the space to cater to large-group events, even integrating the library for events like storytelling, or converting the area into a stage with step seats where an audience can sit to enjoy a small performance. This is enabled by transforming the central staircase into a theater without compromising the function of the vertical circulation; part of the steps functions as seating, from where the audience can view a projection screen that can be lowered across the hall.

Scaled for Children, Remembering Parents

Breaking away from the traditional layout of a children's educational facility—which often arranges closed classrooms and restricts playing to designated play areas—Family Box designs widely spread smart volumes that are filled with a variety of elements to engage children with playing and learning.

Some of these volumes feature slides, climbing zones, upholstered soft seating, bookshelves, and other functional elements, which allow children and guardians to relax with a book or play, wherever and as they like.

These smart volumes are scaled for children to climb, crawl, and walk. Some allow them to explore about together with adults, and some offer the option to take the tour independently, while still maintaining occasional visual contact with their guardians and parents through small square window openings. Such a design extends from the design concept to not only take care of children's needs, but also that of their caretakers, and it also supports the old Chinese philosophy of being close to the family's single child. Instead of a separated waiting zone, the design invites adults into the space (with additional seating around the elevated rooms), and also into the green smart volumes though they are not participating in the activities. Glass walls in the design enable parents and guardians to have a view of the activities their children are engaged in inside the rooms.

1   Waiting area
2   Shoe-changing area
3   Reception
4   Library
5   Reading stage
6   Art room
7   Big blue block room
8   Play tower
9   Cooling station
10 Café
11 Kitchen
12 Baby play area
13 Children's play tower
14 Restroom
15 Office
16 Feeding room
17 Storeroom
18 Party room

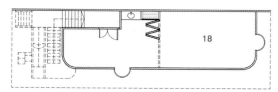

UPPER-FLOOR PLAN

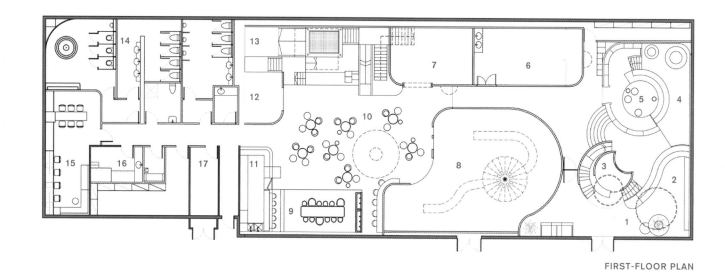

FIRST-FLOOR PLAN

NUBO SYDNEY

LOCATION: SYDNEY,
AUSTRALIA

COMPLETION: 2017

DESIGN: P A L DESIGN
GROUP

PHOTOGRAPHY:
MS. MICHELLE YOUNG,
AMY PIDDINGTON

Nestled within a three-story space in Sydney's Alexandria, NUBO—just as its English translation, "cloud," insinuates—is hard to pin down, given its unlimited potential as a creative hub for learning and exploration. Carefully designed and flexibly suited for children from the ages of two to eight, NUBO offers a stimulating and inclusive learning environment to encourage boundless imagination.

In addition to the playful use of graphics that is completed with warm pastel tones, its well-lit, boundary-free open space emphasizes the concept of "pure play" to make and create—a guiding outlook that becomes inclusive in the children's various stages of learning, so they can safely and curiously explore their surroundings.

With its range of activities categorized traditionally into "active" and "passive" play—the former including slides and nets to climb and scamper about on and the latter encompassing classes conducted in equally immersive environments, that include cake-making and painting—NUBO extends to children opportunities to explore their individual preferences and discover their unique selves.

A warm-white finish, natural lighting, and tables and chairs in a wooden finish, scaled to children's proportions, set up a homey learning environment that is inviting and inclusive. The overall design takes a minimalist approach and removes unnecessary furniture and equipment, incorporating just enough for children to invent their own games.

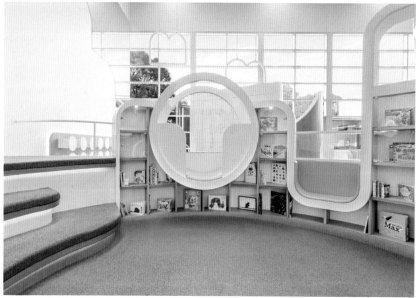

Recognizing that it is equally important to invite parents to spend quality time with their children, the design also considers instances for parents to accompany their children, allowing plenty of interaction between the two. Stations and activities are arranged such that parents can choose to either relax or join in the fun and get in touch with their inner child to learn alongside their children with the same childlike curiosity. In this well-intended space of learning, discovery, and play, the "pure play" concept translates to creating something for everyone to enjoy.

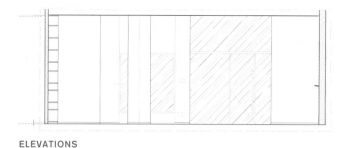 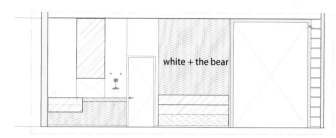

ELEVATIONS

PLAYFUL SPACE

WHITE + THE BEAR

LOCATION: DUBAI,
UNITED ARAB EMIRATES

COMPLETION: 2019

DESIGN: SNEHA DIVIAS
ATELIER

PHOTOGRAPHY:
NATELEE COCKS,
OANA MINUTI

white + the bear is the world's first children's restaurant that offers a healthy and nutritious children-specific menu that has been co-created by world renowned celebrity chef and children's food expert, Annabel Karmel. Designed as a destination for city dwellers seeking a distinct vibe that appeals to children, the restaurant and concept store combination also serves as a resting stop for parents who are out and about with their children.

Owner Hana Al Mula envisioned the concept together with Karmel and the space was brought to life as a result of consistent collaboration and synergy between the design team and clients.

Unlike other child-centered spaces that are characterized by bright colors and pop-culture personalities, white + the bear embraces a unique aesthetic that's urbane and effective for learning.

Spatial Layout
The concept store comprises two floors, which means that there's plenty of space to accommodate children and parents who want to take a break or buy something from a vast collection of products. Both the store and restaurant are blended into each other, such that a distinct transition from one to the other is not obvious, so visitors simply "flow" from one area to the next. Blurred lines between the ground and first floor also help facilitate seamless transitions throughout the space.

On the ground level, the restaurant lies amid the retail section, along with the kitchen and washrooms.

The retail area moves up to the first floor on wooden stairs, and through a black, metal arch that entices the customer to explore and ascend the stairs to the next level. Here, a reading corner and a space for special events, like workshops and birthday parties are made to delight young visitors. It also includes a nursing space and a store. It is intended that young visitors form a deep connection with the design and recognize the space and layout as a safe, easy-to-navigate environment.

Concept
A holistic design delivers all things that parents would want their children to be surrounded by—healthy food, a safe environment, productive learning, and so on. The color theory that is aligned with the graphic design makes up a great part of the design analysis. Hence a neutral color palette is applied, rather than one that would overstimulate children's senses.

The design concept creates a multifaceted experience for children and parents. Children explore different sensory triggers while eating, learning, reading, and exploring, and share these findings with their parents. This also helps improve the interaction between parents and children.

Design Features
To enhance children's creativity and imagination skills, complex strategies are avoided. Instead, clean lines and a minimalist space are iterated, while ensuring a warm atmosphere is retained, courtesy of a distinctive range of textures.

white + the bear

hi, nice
to meet you

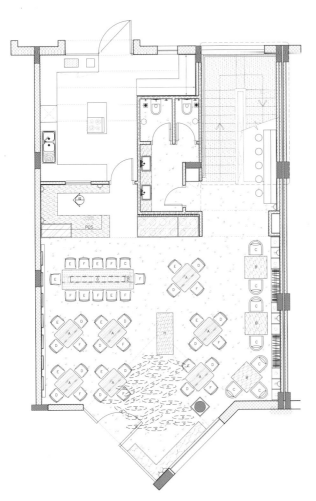

GROUND-FLOOR FURNITURE LAYOUT

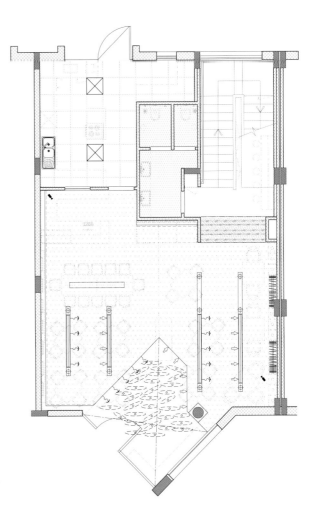

GROUND-FLOOR CEILING LAYOUT

Bespoke full-height shelving to display merchandise, wood slate counters, and a bespoke joinery design that integrates all the elements are some of the key features.

There is also a feature wall with suspended metal hangers that relate the design to the functionality of displaying items. The first floor has a breathable area with glass partitions separating the private rooms from the shop. Throughout the space, playful and quirky graphic elements greet the children and ignite their artistic senses. It also promotes imagination, so they feel inspired by the space and confident about new ideas.

Materials and Furniture

Consistency was important when incorporating a color scheme, keeping in line with the brand story and concept: white and black, minimal, serene, and fresh. A simple material palette is adopted, focusing on elements like lacquer, veneer, metal, Corian, and vinyl flooring. The selection of finishes is based on each treatment's aesthetic appeal, as well as its maintenance requirements.

As visitors enter the premises, an eye-catching installation of hanging bird lights from Brokis welcomes them. Children can get comfortable in the seating area, while parents have their own seating area arranged with Haworth Harbor chairs. The washrooms are ergonomically designed and scaled to children's height, and incorporate washbasins from Cielo and fixtures from Bagno Design. The ceilings are straight and clean, with recessed, black light slots to create lighting that accentuates key elements.

Design Theory

A simple but functional aesthetic prevails in the design, accompanied with wonderful details and honest materiality. The space is divided into partitions, so that the usually fleeting focus and attention of young visitors is easily retained. It also helps each section stand prominently. A sleek white background places retail products at centerstage.

Details such as children's ages were also considered during the design process. As a result, the final product contains numerous opportunities for children of all ages to interact and socialize with

> Workshops
> Party Room
> Reading Nook
> Gift Wrapping
> Concept Store
> Baby Nursing /
> Changing Station

each other. There are spaces to eat, play, read, shop, and simply observe and discover the world.

In today's world, children should be left to explore their surroundings and find their "own space" where they feel comfortable, which is why white + the bear has been designed to contain many of such places where children can find others like them, with similar interests, and make friends. The design humanizes the interior architecture, bringing a sense of proportion and scale, so children feel included.

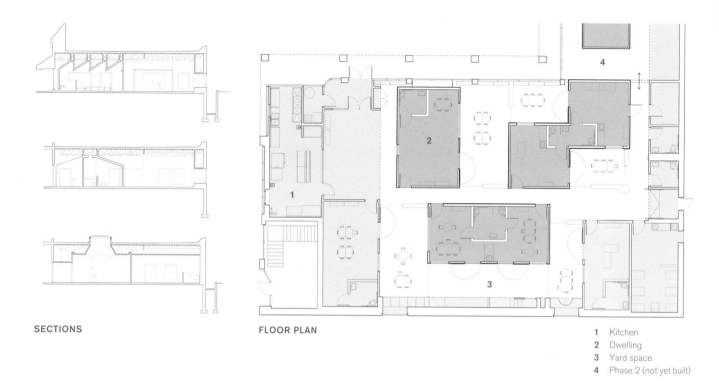

SECTIONS

FLOOR PLAN

1 Kitchen
2 Dwelling
3 Yard space
4 Phase 2 (not yet built)

EDUCATIONAL SPACE

SOLBE LEARNING CENTER

LOCATION: BOSTON,
UNITED STATES

COMPLETION: 2019

DESIGN: SUPERNORMAL

PHOTOGRAPHY:
TRENT BELL

This early learning center design questions the traditional definition of the "classroom," which is commonly interpreted from the general early education code to be a room bounded by four walls, with a space area of 35 square feet (3.3 square meters) per child. Here, the classroom is reimagined as distinct zones of activity with specific spatial characteristics that better match the quality and level of activity within them.

The "dwelling" objects act as islands within the open floor plan to host focused, quiet learning and small group exploration for up to 100 children. The open "yard" space between these dwellings engages children in active play focused on developing gross motor skills, and accommodates the seed-to-table lunchtime curriculum, as well as larger group activities. This oscillation between focused learning and a free play territory creates spaces that are sensitive to the needs of children as they transition through growth stages, reflecting SolBe's innovative curriculum. The spaces also accommodate different

activities for different times of the day. The bold forms of the dwellings encase calm and quiet interiors with indirect lighting. Outside the dwellings, a high ceiling, filled with openings, scatters dappled natural light into the yard through a screen of acoustic baffles, ensuring that the diurnal cycles are felt and observed.

The radical redistribution of the space of the classroom displays impact within the local neighborhood context as well. The gross motor skills area, commercial kitchen, and contiguous yard-like play spaces are used by the extended community for music lessons, winter weekend play, and continuing education during the evenings and weekends when the center's early learning classes are not in session. The space is designed to a variety of user types. Skylights bring natural light deep into the space and maximize the connection to the outdoors. This connection heightens the children's attention to weather and lighting conditions, and the neighborhood around them.

Each classroom functions like a child's home away from home. The diversity of form assigns every classroom a specific identity and the diversity of spatial effect—quiet, peaceful, and neutral in color on the inside, and colorful, active, and engaging on the outside—enables a sense of comfort and helps children feel safe, while making room for exploration.

Children and Their Families

With a "seed to table" curriculum, flexible space, educational programing, and a commercial kitchen to provide dinner and breakfast for two-parent working families, the design acknowledges the complexities of contemporary family life and creates more space and time for parents and caregivers to be with their children.

Teachers and Caregivers

Great care has been given to the design of comfortable and accessible teaching environments to enable teachers and caregivers to thrive. Considerations include increased natural light and optimized visibility within and outside the classrooms.

Local Residents

During working hours on weekdays, the space is designed to conduct early learning and pre-kindergarten classes. In the evenings and weekends, it is opened to the local community. The core elements of the classrooms close and the space in between them transforms into zones for music performances, cooking demonstrations, yoga, and family movie nights, with the goal to create a more integrated and active local community more hours of the day and week.

EL PORVENIR CHILD DEVELOPMENT CENTER

LOCATION: ANTIOQUIA, COLOMBIA

COMPLETION: 2019

DESIGN: TALLER SÍNTESIS

PHOTOGRAPHY: ARQUITECTOS MAURICIO CARVAJAL

The El Porvenir Child Development Center is a public institution located in the municipality of Rionegro, Antioquia, Colombia. The center serves the immediate and surrounding neighborhoods and can house up to a total of 400 children at one time.

The new headquarters replaces a smaller previous building with a single-level brick building made up of a series of vaulted pavilions that project toward the Malpaso ravine and a forest that has been planted as part of the reconstruction to support sustainability.

Pavilions house classrooms that have a direct link with a series of courtyards. This not only builds in adequate ventilation and lighting, but also enables a direct relationship between the children and nature, giving the landscape a permanent presence in the educational spaces, while facilitating the effective integration of the classrooms with nature.

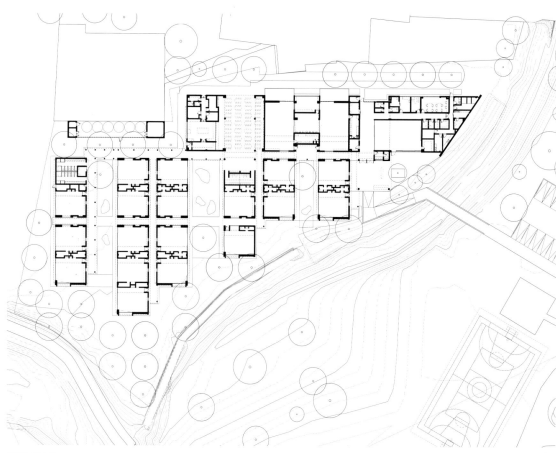

SITE PLAN

ELEVATIONS

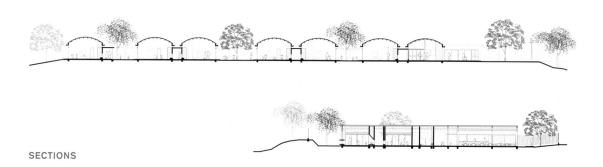

SECTIONS

The pavilions are joined by a perpendicularly set volume that houses the collective areas of the project: a canteen that functions as a large, covered courtyard, administration facilities, services for parents and students, an auditorium that opens directly to the exterior to allow the community use of the facilities, and a covered hall where parents can wait for their children and not have to worry about the weather.

The tailoring of the scale to children's size is observed throughout the facility, appearing in niches, windows, and furniture that are arranged at their height, so as to allow children to build their own landscape that is available only to them. The color treatment of each of the rooms also gives them a particular character that allows children to identify them easily; it also facilitates the appropriation of each space.

EDUCATIONAL SPACE

HELLO BABY

LOCATION: DNIPRO,
UKRAINE

COMPLETION: 2020

DESIGN: SVOYA STUDIO

PHOTOGRAPHY:
ALEXANDER ANGELOVSKYI

Hello BABY is located on the first floor of a
residential complex in the central part of the city
of Dnipro in Ukraine. The project begun as an
initiative to design a new additional space for the
existing center, but with a separate identity. In the
process, a new name and branding were developed
for the center as a whole, resulting in a new design
concept for the entire center.

With an area of 5,565 square feet (517 square
meters), the center includes the following groups
of rooms:

• The entrance group combines a reception, a mini
coffee house and a store retailing themed products.
From this space there is an exit to a corridor that
runs through the entire center. This provides for the
prospect of expanding the space in the future. The
corridor has a game function and is equipped with
stylized seating.

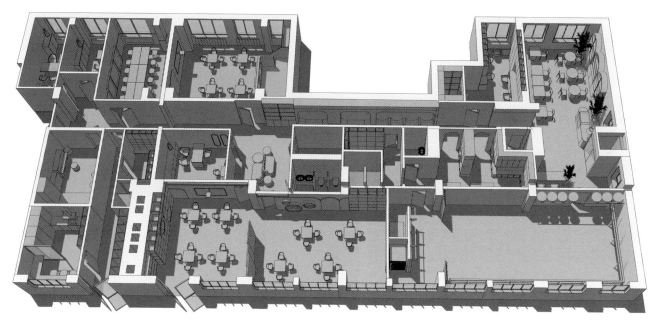

DIAGRAM

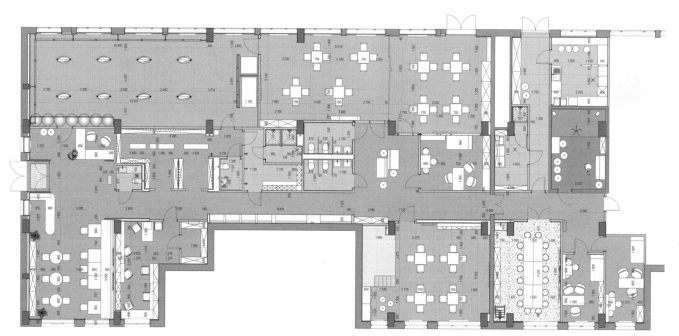

FLOOR PLAN

• The gym is accessed from the reception and the changing rooms. The gym accommodates both children's classes and parents' classes, having a separate adult locker room with showers.

• The office for administration and teachers is also located as close as possible to the entrance area.

• The center features separate restrooms for children, adults, and staff, with attached shower facilities.

• There are three large classrooms, two of which can be combined, and with one adapted for "quiet hour."

• The facility also includes a music room and a room for creative activities and crafts.

The design pays attention to a convenient scheme of interconnection within the premises and the transition from one space to the next, as well as the possibility of future expansion.

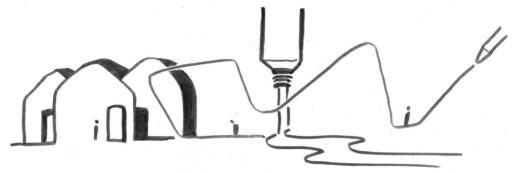

52 ARTS

LOCATION: SHENZHEN, CHINA

COMPLETION: 2018

DESIGN: P A L DESIGN GROUP

PHOTOGRAPHY: DICK LIU

52 Arts is a creative studio that caters to children from three to twelve years old with a welcoming, fun, and flexible space accommodated to host a comprehensive range of art classes for western painting, Chinese painting, pottery, and crafts. Both purpose-driven and mentally stimulating, the design presents kids and adults alike with an unexpected spatial experience to inspire creativity and beauty, in line with the principles of the school.

The journey begins with a well-lit, bright, and welcoming entrance inspired by drawing tools, and which is expressed in warm pastel colors. The central structural column is sculpted as an adorable and eye-catching floor-height plump paintbrush, in complement to another slender paintbrush that has its white brush tip "painting" a band feature that links the reception and the kid's gallery, extending across the interiors as a tube-like design feature.

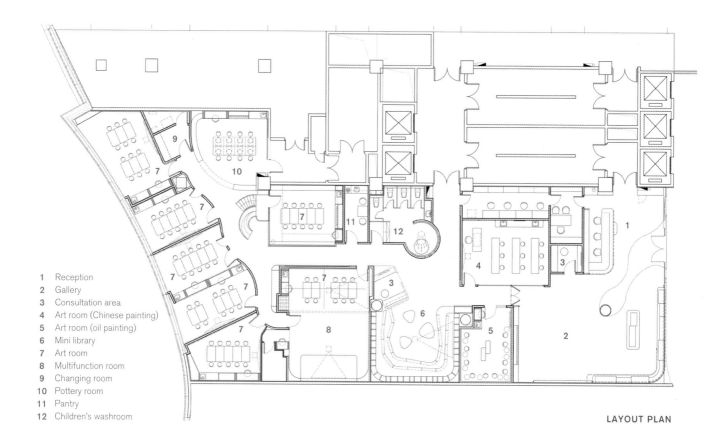

1   Reception
2   Gallery
3   Consultation area
4   Art room (Chinese painting)
5   Art room (oil painting)
6   Mini library
7   Art room
8   Multifunction room
9   Changing room
10 Pottery room
11 Pantry
12 Children's washroom

LAYOUT PLAN

The emphasis is on a holistic development that focuses on the being as a whole, and toward that arranges corresponding spaces which can facilitate classes that encourage both individual and group learning. Drawing inspiration from galleries, the welcome lounge showcases completed masterpieces of the center's students in a bright, carefree space that prepares them for the journey of discovery that awaits within.

Vibrant wooden houses form a nurturing ground for free-thinking individuals, while open spaces encourage conversation and the exchange of ideas among children, parents, and teachers. Adding to that, a library offers an airy reading environment and also hosts storytelling sessions that are imaginatively lit by translucent "flying books," creating a magical and engaging space fit for these story world sessions.

Lovely surprises await even in the washroom, where a custom-made design feature overhead appears like a tipped over bucket of water, highlighting the space while stimulating the children's curiosity, so as to invite them to interact with the space. Sleek, curving walls wrap around and meander throughout the interiors to add another layer of visual dynamism in the interior.

The concept and vision of 52 Arts is to reward children with fruitful moments of boundless creativity, instead of them having to endure the drudgery of a typical after-school class in a traditional, rigid teacher-versus-student setting. Here, they develop their full potential in an open, stress-free, and safe learning environment that allows them to bring fantasy to life and fill their world with favorites.

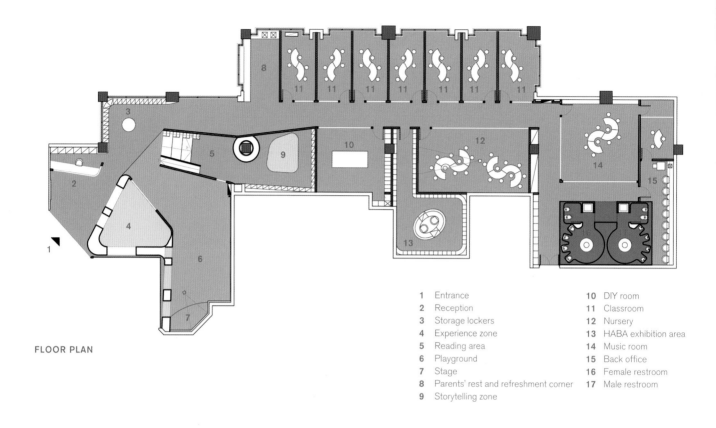

FLOOR PLAN

1	Entrance	10	DIY room
2	Reception	11	Classroom
3	Storage lockers	12	Nursery
4	Experience zone	13	HABA exhibition area
5	Reading area	14	Music room
6	Playground	15	Back office
7	Stage	16	Female restroom
8	Parents' rest and refreshment corner	17	Male restroom
9	Storytelling zone		

PLAYPLUS

LOCATION: SHENZHEN, CHINA

COMPLETION: 2016

DESIGN: PANORAMA DESIGN GROUP

PHOTOGRAPHY: NG SIU FUNG

PlayPlus is a playful and exciting environment that carries out the kindergarten's mission to nurture children that can think, learn, and act independently. The overall space is a design metaphor of an abstract "landscape," in which different degrees of openness, scales, heights, and proportions are manipulated, so that they can be experienced to the fullest by the children, to cater to their different activity needs for reading, drawing, playing, classroom-learning, and story time.

The key zones in classrooms, the playground, reading corner, and washrooms are finished in timber veneer and are complemented with pastel-colored upholsteries to express dynamic, vivid, and inspiring learning environments that promote mutual interaction.

Feature walls that present multimedia projections are juxtaposed with traditional chalkboards to provide flexible and tactile teaching media for teachers. Floating logo-inspired cross-shaped lights organize the spatial directory and complete children's fantasy of the space.

WEGROW

LOCATION: NEW YORK,
UNITED STATES

COMPLETION: 2018

DESIGN: BJARKE INGELS
GROUP (BIG)

PHOTOGRAPHY:
DAVE BURK,
LAURIAN GHINITOIU

The interactive learning landscape of WeGrow supports a conscious approach to education, nurturing the growth, spirit, and mind of the twenty-first-century child. This 10,000 square-foot (929-square-meter) learning universe for children aged three to nine, located in WeWork's headquarters in Manhattan's Chelsea neighborhood, is inspired by a belief in creativity.

A range of spaces with a variety of functions allows children to move freely throughout the day and to learn from the environment around them, and each other. The learning landscape encourages collaboration by emphasizing transparent and communal spaces, which comprise more than half of the school, making up four classrooms, flexible workshops, a community space, multipurpose studio, art studio, music room, and other playscapes that support the energy of creation and togetherness.

Most of the partitions inside the school are designed as shelves that are kept at the height of a child, allowing natural light to reach deep inside the building. Three different shelving levels are created for each age group of children and curve occasionally to design various activity pockets in the space that impart a feeling of comfort and safety, while facilitating a community ambiance. The low shelves also allow teachers to have full perspective of the space at all times. Above, clouds made of felt reflect different patterns in nature—fingerprints, corals, landscapes, and the moon—and illuminate the space with Ketra bulbs that shift in color and intensity based on the time of day.

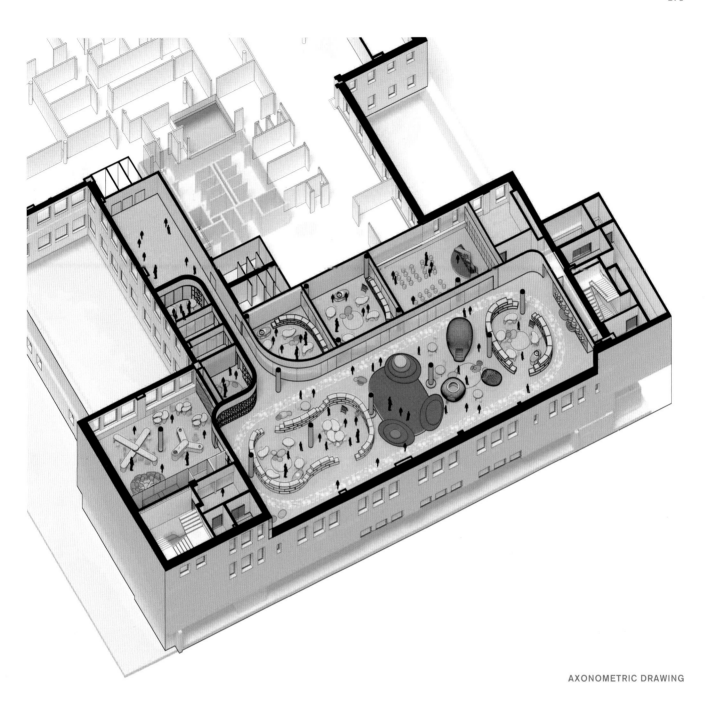

AXONOMETRIC DRAWING

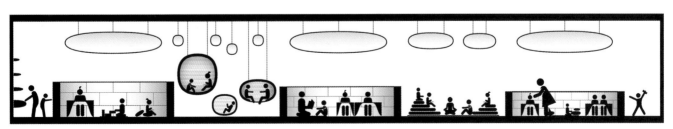

PERSPECTIVE DIAGRAM

Each learning station within WeGrow features furniture with details and materials that are carefully designed to optimize the educational environment: modular classrooms promote movement and collaboration; puzzle tables and chairs manufactured by Bendark Studios come in kid and parent sizes to offer equal perspectives; and the vertical garden with tiles made in Switzerland by Laufen houses different plants. The mushroom shelves and magic meadow create a calm setting for more focused study, while reading hives form an immersive library for an organic learning environment.

Teachers and parents share the lobby with the children, where a wall cutout forms a playful nook fashioned in felt, which serves as a flexible work, meet, and waiting area. Children can also try their hand at the brain puzzle, which is in fact the all-felt lounge, which can be taken apart for playing and learning.

From the lobby to the classrooms, WeGrow is lit by the Gople Lamp and Alphabet of Light flexible lighting systems designed by BIG Ideas and manufactured by Artemide, to create ambiance effects that form comfortable, natural lighting throughout the school day. Playful and transparent, yet homelike and structured, WeGrow nurtures the child's education through introspection, exploration, and discovery.

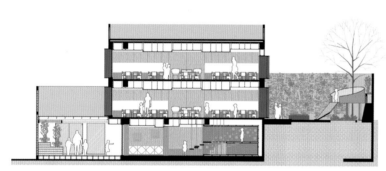

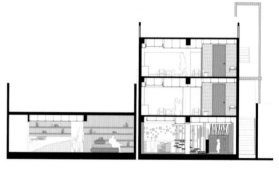

SECTIONS

NIA SCHOOL

LOCATION: MEXICO CITY, MEXICO

COMPLETION: 2019

DESIGN: SULKIN ASKENAZI

PHOTOGRAPHY: ALDO C. GRACIA

Nia School is a 6,458-square-foot (600-square-meter) learning space that aims to unlock the creative potential of children between two and eight years old through design, which is achieved by supporting the growth of children through environments that allow them to develop their skills through interactive learning.

The field allows children to move freely between the various flexible spaces; the stage presents a space for movement to exercise the body and mind; and two learning rooms integrate nature into the interior design. Lighting systems are designed to create a comfortable and natural environment that is conducive to hosting a range of activities.

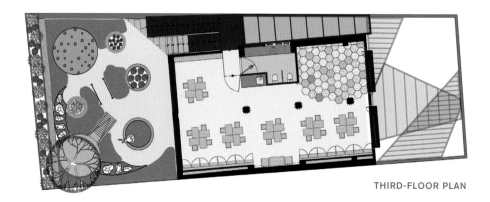

THIRD-FLOOR PLAN

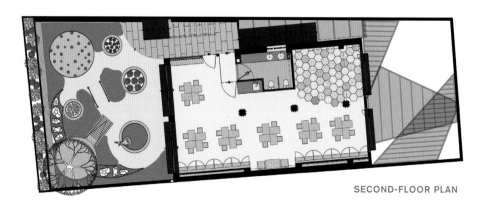

SECOND-FLOOR PLAN

FIRST-FLOOR PLAN

The reception has ergonomic furniture for children, including wooden buds, seats that reflect nature, and shelves at different heights that allow the space to perform as a learning station at all times. Geometric wooden modules design shelves in the classrooms to house learning material, and which also function as a passive learning system themselves through their interesting shapes. Warm reading spaces with hexagonal rugs patterned like a beehive complete the interior installations and

create an open learning environment. The emerging collaboration hall behind the central corridor is expressed as a game environment, enhancing exploration and discovery. The living room has softer touches, such as cork and oak.

The color-blocking approach—with only intermittent pops of baby blue—was crucial to make the space inviting to children, while also triggering education and exploration. It is the hope that the design and concept will instill a unique appreciation for design in the young minds of the children of Mexico City.

EDUCATIONAL SPACE

LITTLE HIGH KIDS SCHOOL

LOCATION: GYEONGGI-DO,
SOUTH KOREA

COMPLETION: 2018

DESIGN: MINGSHEN,
SOLBIN JEON / M4

PHOTOGRAPHY: STUDIO
770, JAESANG LEE

A recent commercial in Korea has been resonating deeply and identifying closely with many tired, worn-out parents missing their zeal for parenting. It begins with a mother reading her son a bedtime story about dinosaurs. When the boy is fast asleep, she mischievously reveals: "Actually, Mommy doesn't like dinosaurs. Mommy likes romance stories," and she starts reading romance webtoons on her phone. The tagline then appears to ring home the gist of the message: be happy, even if it is just for a moment.

This commercial has been running on an online platform and many parents who watch it relate closely with it, remarking, "That is exactly how I feel and what I want to say!"

It is said, Korean moms and dads have such a busy life that they don't even have time to look in the mirror; this commercial reminds them not to give up on happiness, reflecting the social phenomenon of the times, which says that present society no longer requires the unconditional sacrifice of parents. In fact, many parents agree that the best

education for children these days is showing them that their parents are happy. Taking a page from that book, early childhood education these days advocates scenarios where both parents and children are happy.

Extending on that, for this project, the team considered a place where both parents and kids can be happy and thought hard about what it should look like; what stories, themes, and features should be conceptualized and executed in such a place? The result is a children-centered environment that pursues experience and education.

The client, a father of two, sought to provide a valuable experience for both parents and children in one place. He wanted to create a place that offers a value beyond just entertainment. Little High Kids School, a kids café, aims to be a complex facility where visitors can engage in activities that are usually provided in English kindergartens or playschools. Children can have great fun, and parents can also take some time to relax.

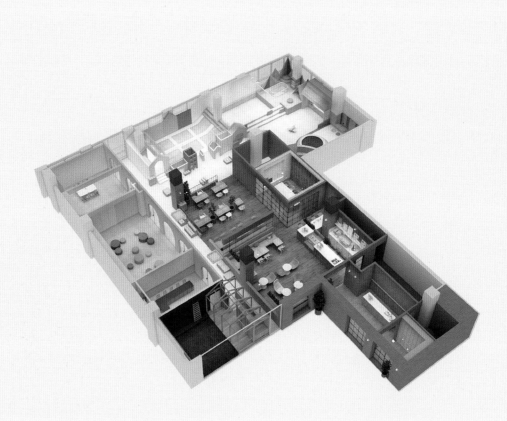

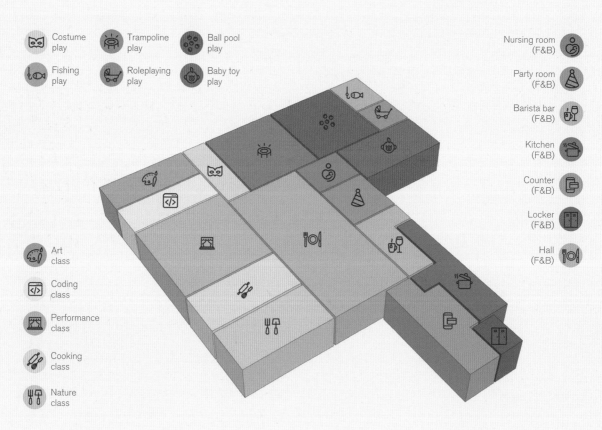

Costume play

Trampoline play

Ball pool play

Fishing play

Roleplaying play

Baby toy play

Art class

Coding class

Performance class

Cooking class

Nature class

Nursing room (F&B)

Party room (F&B)

Barista bar (F&B)

Kitchen (F&B)

Counter (F&B)

Locker (F&B)

Hall (F&B)

Finding the Spatial Motif in Human Self-fantasy

Everyone wants to find their true identity and live their own life, having a desire to pursue the pleasure of finding their inner self. This is the same for both young children at their early development stages, as well as adults who have children of their own. For adults, it is usually when they are taking a break from the responsibilities of parenthood that they reminisce about their younger days and their "forgotten self" whom they traded for the responsible, hardworking parent that they now are. As for children, they enjoy playing and learning, and see a new side of themselves in a world of imagination, and create their own fantasy.

Therefore, the design motif in the space makes room for "self-fantasy" and transports both parents and children into a place of happiness, where they can each, respectively, dream, reminisce, and imagine.

Accompanying Adults Can be Invaluable Guests

To start, the team considered the type of "dreams" that parents might have. Being a parent is highly rewarding, but it often means caring less about oneself. Almost every aspect of life is focused on the child, with parents' personal preferences being put aside. To cater an inviting space for parents, the task of "relaxing" from parents' perspectives was carefully deliberated.

In the F&B area, adult preferences and lifestyles are given importance, instead of simply creating an area with food and an interior tailored only to kids.

However, a place with kids will hardly be free from noise and distraction. Therefore, a party concept—with loud music, chatting, mingling, and interacting—was tailored to allow some leeway for the bustle and hype to become a part of the experience and enjoyment. This vibrant and lively atmosphere is directed to a rooftop location that successfully executes a rooftop party concept, with detailed design elements that carry the idea through.

To emphasize the natural openness of a rooftop, green plants and low stone wall partitions, bricks, and wood decking are used. The soft, comfortable sofas and dim lighting make a cozy place for a chat, and parents can let their hair down and enjoy the food, music, and friendly conversation in a lively atmosphere.

A Playground Where Children Can Explore Their Potential and Grow

Play Zone is a land where infinite fantasies come true. Clouds in different shapes reflect typical aspirations of children and express an atmosphere of hope and ideals, empowering children to discover their full potential. In this cloud land, abundant dreams flutter across a blue sky of possibilities.

This zone is designed to fulfill the fantasy of a "limitless space," taking into account that growing kids are keen to test their physical limits.

Accordingly, physical activities are divided into four main categories: Power—encompassing activities of throwing, hitting, and kicking; Fast—consisting activities of running and jumping; High—with exciting activities like hanging and climbing; and Relaxed—with activities that center on swimming and floating.

The space is designed to allow children to safely partake in these activities without limits. Consistency is also maintained in the design by creating each activity area in the image of buildings and mountaintops that peek through clouds.

Explore Zone promotes the ideal, "be myself." In this area, children can engage in activities to discover their interests and talents. Folding doors facilitate various programs and spatial divisions effectively, tailoring the space to the number of participants.

Children can try on costume uniforms of different professions and use toys and props associated with these professions to play pretend and develop positive aspirations about their future.

The overall atmosphere is very bright, in contrast to the F&B area, where parents mostly spend the time.

When the kids enter the F&B area from the Play or Explore Zones, the change in the ambiance is noticeable, unconsciously cuing them to tone down loud, excited voices and boisterous behavior.

People Gather Around the Warmth of an Everlasting Bonfire

Kevin Kelley, the co-founder of the American design firm Shook Kelley, once spoke of "the bonfire effect" in a talk, sharing his secret to turning commercial and retail environments, such as stores, into gathering places. Drawing a relation, he explained how people naturally gather around a bonfire when camping to exchange

greetings, chat with each other, and share in the warm, convivial ambiance; the bonfire builds a special bond between people. So, when there is a subject of common interest—like a figurative bonfire—in a meeting place, people naturally get together around it to enjoy that special unity.

Little High Kids School aims to be acknowledged as a venue that fulfills the individual needs of parents and children, while promoting their unique values. It is a place that offers its own unique version of the bonfire, and it is the hope that the flames of joy in this bonfire never burn out.

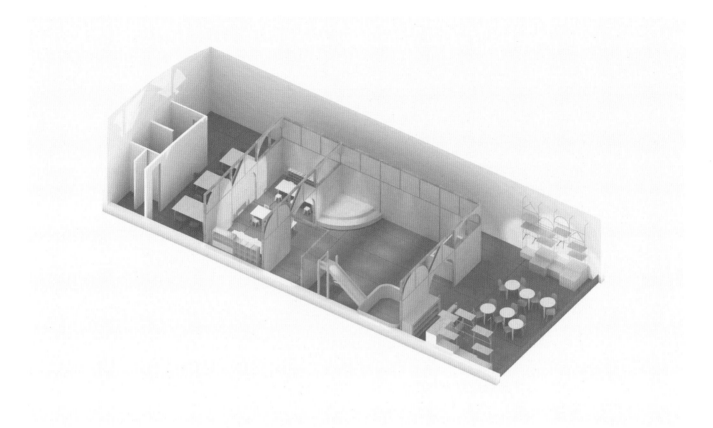

AXONOMETRIC DRAWING

PARENT-CHILD SPACE

BIG AND TINY

<u>LOCATION:</u> SANTA MONICA, LOS ANGELES, UNITED STATES

<u>COMPLETION:</u> 2018

<u>DESIGN:</u> ZOOCO ESTUDIO

<u>PHOTOGRAPHY:</u> AARON & JON PHOTOGRAPHERS

The idea of Big and Tiny was born out of the need to design a venue for both kids and adults to enjoy; a place where families can grow in every aspect of their lives.

This first center under the brand is located in Santa Monica, Los Angeles, United States and offers a unique enrichment space that fosters productivity, creativity, and a sense of community for both parents and kids. It is the first integrated learn, play, and work space with entrepreneurial parents in mind, that brings the flexibility of traditional coworking spaces to childcare.

The mission of the company is to support and empower its vibrant community of parents by helping them integrate their personal and professional lives. Based on this, Big and Tiny was designed with both adults and children in mind.

The facility's high wooden bow truss ceiling extends its 2,100-square-foot (95-square-meter) space transversely. These trusses divide the space into three separate areas, with the middle being the predominant space.

The front space features a coffee and retail area, while the middle core area functions as a playground for kids. The most secluded third area serves as a coworking space for adults.

Using the original truss ceiling as an example of a universal geometric language, a repetitive modular and constructive system is created, reminiscent of a puzzle. This adaptable system creates appealing elevations in all three areas.

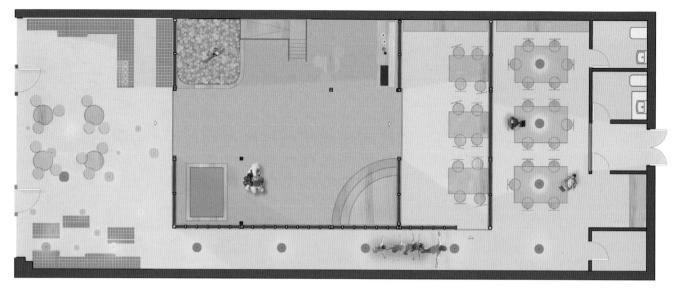

FLOOR PLAN

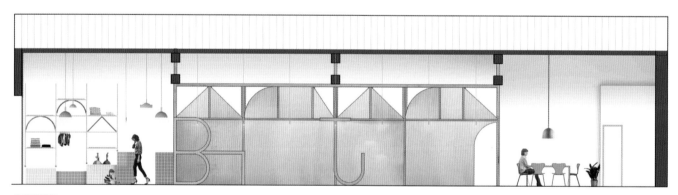

SECTION

The front reception/retail area is a multipurpose space with bespoke iron rack installations on the walls that navigate to a counter in the back. Modular and movable merchandise display cubes made out of 4-by-4-inch (10-by-10-centimeter) pink and blue ceramic tiles reflect the brand colors and offer the flexibility to configure the space according to different needs.

The main central space (the middle core) is presented inside a large wooden structure and divided in two parts. The playground, Tinyland, includes wooden play structures, such as the ball pit and a slide, and the art studio provides a space for children to work on their art projects and attend enrichment classes.

The third and final area, located between the big wooden structure and the outdoor patio, accommodates coworking facilities for parents. The space features office furniture from Normann Cophenhagen, as well as a soundproof phone booth by ROOM.

BIG AND TINY SILVERLAKE

LOCATION: SILVERLAKE, LOS ANGELES, UNITED STATES

COMPLETION: 2019

DESIGN: ZOOCO ESTUDIO

PHOTOGRAPHY: PIXEL LAB

This Big and Tiny project in Silverlake, Los Angeles, United States is the second establishment opened under the brand umbrella; the first was opened in Santa Monica, Los Angeles.

The project occupies a 5,026.7-square-foot (467-square-meter) area, with a maximum height of 21.3 feet (6.5 meters), and which is characterized by a visible roof structure of wooden trusses that covers the entire factory building, exempting the interior space of needing structural walls. The building

features a few closed volumes in different heights that contain maintenance functions, restrooms, a kitchen, and meeting rooms.

The premises have been constructed on a two-prong strategy: The first is to generate two different spaces acoustically isolated from each other, for adults and children respectively. The second is to create open squares in both spaces by compressing the private uses in the volumes that are ordered around these squares.

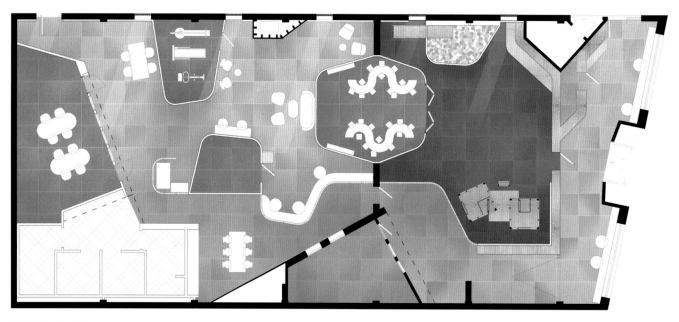

FLOOR PLAN

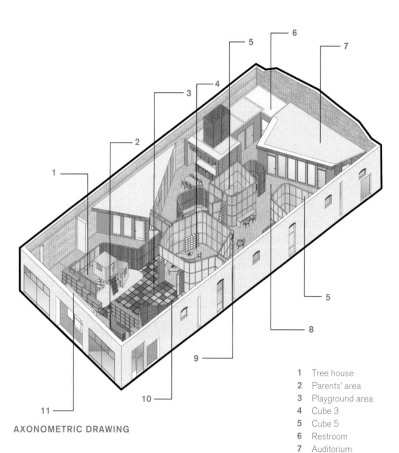

AXONOMETRIC DRAWING

1 Tree house
2 Parents' area
3 Playground area
4 Cube 3
5 Cube 5
6 Restroom
7 Auditorium
8 Coworking area
9 Living room area
10 Cube 2
11 Hall

A wall that splits the building into two parts manifests the acoustic isolation. It is covered by mirrors, so as to generate more amplitude in both spaces. Once this division was implemented, a constructive module is repeated in the form of bands that expand and compress across the span of the spaces, covering the entire perimeter. This spatial tension creates interior spaces that respond to the requested program, while creating the façade of the square that will be the main space for children's activities. Materials like wood, mirror, cork, felt, and cardboard express quality and make up the main interior palette. Wood as a structural element, and in the furniture, generates substance and warmth; the mirror in the central wall amplifies the children and adult spaces; and cork and felt are used as an exterior skin in cubes and baseboards. Cork is also used in the counter and in the exhibition shelves as a way to organize and support the shelves.

In terms of function, two cubed volumes are built inside the children's area (Tree House and Ball Pit) and the adult zone (Bike Cube and Silence Cube) each and one cubed volume is set in between the two areas and connected to the children's area to be used for children's parties. Every cube is connected through high baseboards or curves made of wooden slats. The studs are used as structure in the cavity walls and as independent slats in the connection curves, rendering the module visible in every wall.

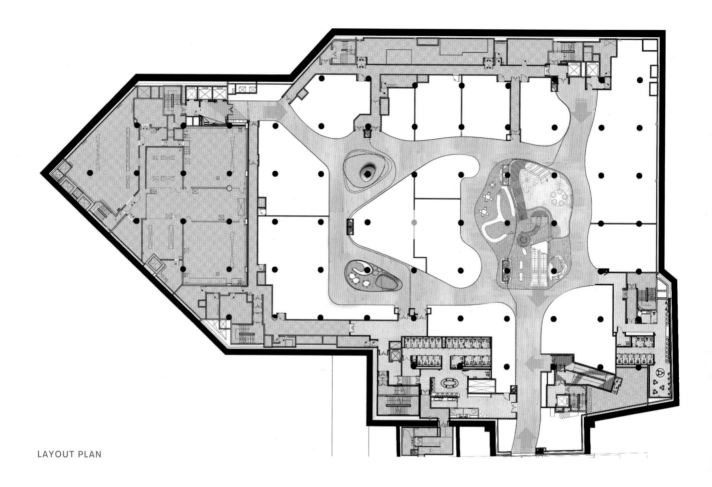

LAYOUT PLAN

PARENT-CHILD SPACE

K11 MUSEA DONUT PLAYHOUSE

LOCATION: HONG KONG,
CHINA

COMPLETION: 2019

INTERIOR DESIGN:
PANORAMA DESIGN GROUP

DESIGN DIRECTOR:
HORACE PAN

PHOTOGRAPHY:
NG SIU FUNG

K11 MUSEA Donut Playhouse is located in the heart of Hong Kong within a composite shopping center. Spanning three stories and connected by giant slides, this playhouse is designed to be the very first kids-oriented play, edutainment, and shopping arcade in the city.

Divided into three main zones—Body, Mind, and Soul—the design of Donut Playhouse manipulates the basic element of point, line, and plane, from the simple perspective of a child, to support the different function and program assigned to each zone. There is a space for exercise (Body), a space for learning (Mind), and a space for performance (Soul).

The children's development is nurtured through introspection, exploration, and discovery, by enhancing their physical, mental, and spiritual quality. All facilities, including the concierge, seating, and directory are catered to ergonomics for children. In the family washrooms, washing islands and cubicles are designed to both the scale of adults and children for convenience and comfort. In the male washroom, specifically, a special "co-wee-wee" zone provides a user-friendly, fun, and unexpected experience on a perfunctory routine act to help foster a closer bond between father and son.

Body: Physical and Active

The energetic and organic Body (play) zone and family café is tuned to unleash energy, encourage a physical workout, and provide a space to relax and recharge. Both lighting and color work hand-in-hand here; the bright atmosphere creates a joyful and active ambiance, while a yellow interior effectively stimulates muscle and encourages hand and foot coordination development of children.

Mind: Mental and Calm

The Mind zone is designed as an open learning hub, where workshops and lessons are made available to parents and kids. The interior scape is selected in green to have an effect of stimulating the memory. Small-sized seats and tables in different shapes provide flexibility to cater to different activities; kids can also sit freely on the padded seats in the reading area, adding fun to their learning.

Soul: Ego and Interactive

The Soul zone contains a mirrored tree as a display structure that displays artwork on a digial carousel. When parents and kids complete their art projects in the workshops, their work will be posted on the platform. Children can then view their work and the works of their fellow little artists and writers. Displaying the children's work in this way helps build their confidence and it also creates an identity with their artwork.

Donut Playhouse believes that a children's arcade should ideally not be just a theme park, but go beyond reality to provide spatial experiences that unleash imaginations. In this one-of-a-kind kid scape for edu-shopping, a sense of magic and playfulness is also incorporated to build a memorable experience of fun, excitement, and bonding for children and parents.

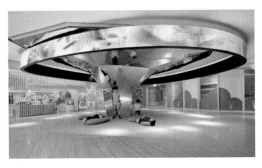

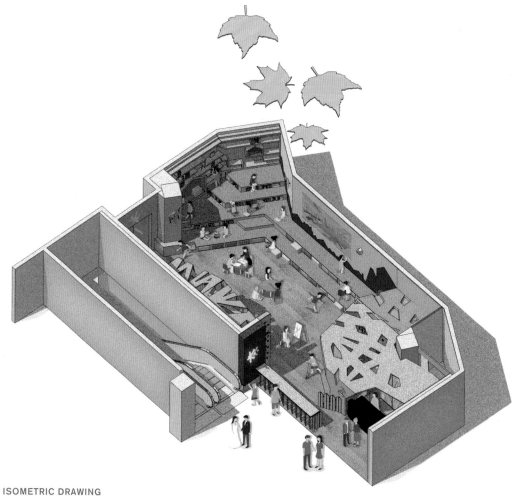

ISOMETRIC DRAWING

KERRYON LIVING ROOM

LOCATION: SHANGHAI, CHINA

COMPLETION: 2018

DESIGN: SPARK

PHOTOGRAPHY: LIU CHE

Pudong KerryOn Living Room is presented as a parent-child social space for KerryOn members. The 1,292-square-foot (120-square-meter) space, located at B1 of Pudong Kerry Shopping Mall, draws inspiration from enchanted forests in fairytales, and is designed to stimulate curiosity, a sense of fun, and interaction among children, as well as between children and their parents.

This idea of the Living Room stems from KerryOn's strategy to remain relevant in the face of disruptive online/offline shopping competition, by creating varied physical experiences that add value for their member shoppers.

Living Room is a place for gathering, a space for parents to spend time with their children, and a place for workshops and events. Spatial flexibility, mobility,

and privacy were key considerations in integrating and layering key functions, such as the concierge, event space, library, parents' zone, and washrooms.

This children's garden of curiosities is set in a simulated "forest clearing" and is surrounded by three-dimensional tree-house stages for curated events. The space is illuminated by a canopy of large backlit tree leaves and colorful forest birds sitting on branches. The forest floor is lined with child-friendly stepped seating that also houses space for books and cushions tailored in KerryOn's brand colors. These colors, in hues of orange, yellow, blue, and green, are used throughout the Living Room to convey the spirit of fun and excitement, and present Living Room as an engaging and fun-filled place to visit.

Activities like parent-child yoga, art and craft workshops, movie screenings, and marketing product launches are held in the forest clearing. A large artwork and projection wall faces the clearing and is visible from the entrance—strategically placed to kindle the curiosity of passers-by.

Tree Houses

The Open House, which is positioned at the separating threshold of the living room and the shopping mall, houses the concierge, storeroom, and washroom. A privacy screen, formed by a "forest fence," integrates shoe storage (which also doubles as a support for leaning against),

a reading area, and phone-charging station to offer some simple services to parents while they wait for their children. The "parents' menagerie" terraced seating, with locker storage, is a space where parents can watch, as well as engage with their children participating in activities. The area also contains an information panel on Living Room and a vending machine.

Learning House is an extension of the terrace seating around the forest clearing and is the most private space within Living Room, with a shelf library and reading nooks finished in padded fabrics to create an inviting and cozy environment.

Forest Fauna and Flora

The layout, scale, and detail of KerryOn Living Room are designed ergonomically, prioritizing child safety, together with the ease of adult monitoring. The enchanted forest theme is applied across the spatial planning and design detailing, highlighting timber textures that feature across the majority of the interior, with contrasting tactile expressions in the lively brand colors of orange, yellow, green, and blue.

The tree houses are designed with abstracted silhouette cutouts of tree scapes, and are detailed with forest bird lights and mini versions of tree houses (house-shaped frames) that camouflage functional devices.

A playful glowing KerryOn supergraphic "K" greets passers-by on the outside of the Living Room, welcoming members into the enchanted forest to experience a culturally enriched day out at the mall. Inspired by Henri Rousseau's sometimes quirky, childlike paintings of exotic landscapes, KerryOn Living Room aims to reflect an environment that will be exciting and inspiring for young children.

MEMO PARENT-CHILD PARTY READING CLUB

LOCATION: NINGBO, ZHEJIANG PROVINCE, CHINA

COMPLETION: 2019

DESIGN: H.G.S DESIGN

PHOTOGRAPHY: PU YAN

"Ten years of planting wood, one year of planting grain, all pay children."

– Yuan Haowen

The brief for this project triggered the recollection of a poem by Yuan Haowen, a poet from then Xinzhou, China. The poem's message expresses how, overall, all of humankind's efforts in most things are, essentially, directed toward the betterment of the lives and living comfort of the next generation.

Inspired by this, the design concept focuses on sculpting space, and induces it with an artistic flair

to anchor the design and form an environment that is interesting to children. The space is divided into an upper and lower layer, using colors and wood to define dynamic and passive areas.

On the first floor, a large area with colored geometric shapes makes the space dynamic and agile, so that children can release their creative ideas; this space also stimulates their natural instincts. In the recreation area, the banana slide combines with creative lighting—placed in the hollow of steps—to keep children's interest and maintain engagement.

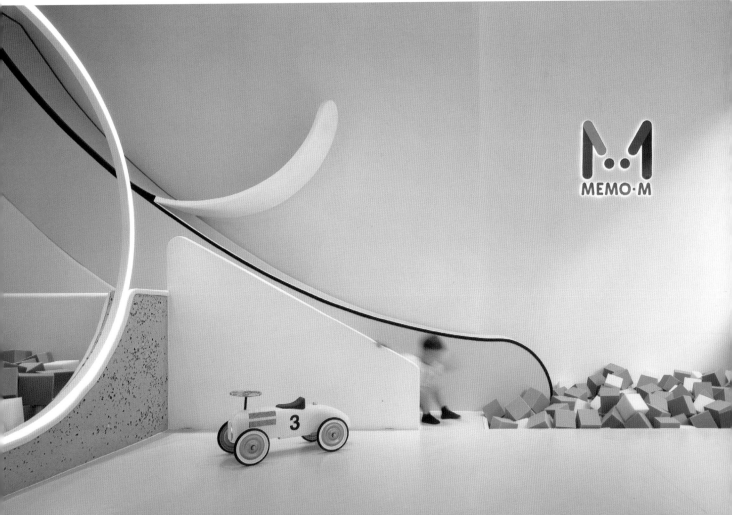

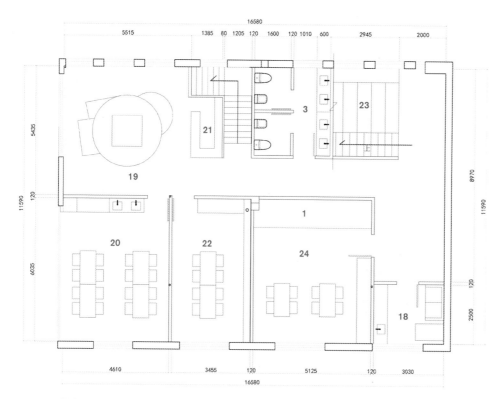

SECOND-FLOOR PLAN

1 Stage
2 Banquet hall
3 Restrooms
4 Dry zone
5 Storeroom
6 Equipment room
7 Reception
8 Parents' area
9 Cooking area
10 Western kitchen
11 Cold kitchen
12 Food prep/chopping area
13 Operation/cleaning room
14 Ball pit
15 Kids' play area
16 Short slide
17 Long slide
18 Baby care room
19 Leisure area
20 Workshop
21 Counter
22 Storybook room
23 Stepped storybook area
24 Theater

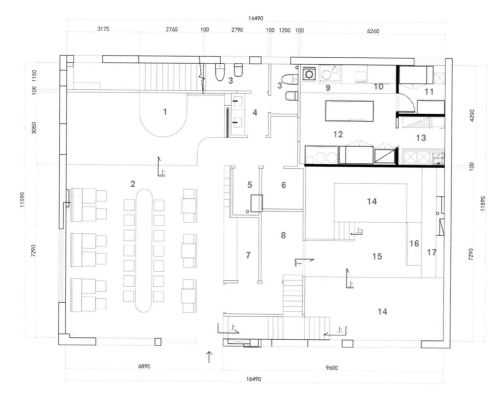

FIRST-FLOOR PLAN

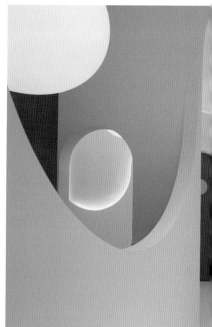

On the second floor, a white color palette is used, together with wooden installations that feature exaggerated curved lines and circular, spherical shapes rather than sharp, straight lines or pointed edges, to create a relaxed and inviting ambiance that is calming and de-stressing, to help children wind down and cool-off after vigorous play. Giant ball lights and tunnel-like corridors are used to dissipate active, hyper energies and calm the mind and connect it to the awareness of presence and self within the environment, and to also align mind and body with relaxation, so that children can gradually transition from a state of excitability to calm.

In this reading club, color and shapes are used to speak to children's innate nature to help them form an understanding of the environment and their response to it.

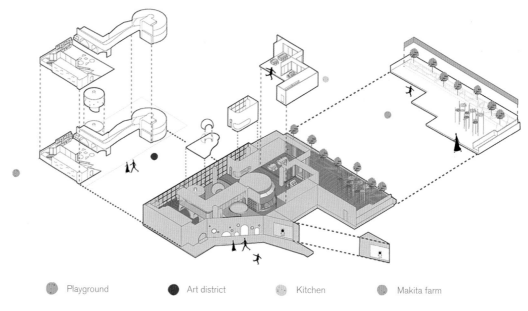

⬤ Playground   ⬤ Art district   ⬤ Kitchen   ⬤ Makita farm

AXONOMETRIC DRAWING

STAR ART HOME

LOCATION: CHONGQING, CHINA

COMPLETION: 2018

DESIGN: ITD STUDIO

PHOTOGRAPHY: LIU YUJIE

Star Art Home is a multifunctional children's facility that combines a family restaurant, an art exhibition space, and a recreation facility with abstract sculptural installations designed around a space adventure concept, to tailor a unique imaginative world that supports creativity, development, confidence-building, and a curiosity to explore. The engaging space adventure storyline and design concept were formed based on children's natural instinct for play, and aim to unlock their innate nature, as well as provide them infinite room for imagination and creation. The dining environment, and its effect on the physical and psychological health of children was also closely considered, as were building guidelines and the requirements of the property's owner.

The main highlights of this galaxy wonderland feature the following design modules:

1. A beacon and a dark space
A 134-square-foot (13-square-meter) enclosed, dark, circular module, also known as the dark space, on the second floor features forty-three openings through which children can observe the world from different angles. The space also inspires children to imagine that they are floating in the dark galaxy, the illuminated circular openings as planets or drifting

asteroids. The scenarios that little minds can conjure here are limited only by their imaginations.

2. Half-moon cosplay theater
This semicircular cave-like cocoon set under the bridge, measuring 570.5 square feet (53 square meters), is finished in yellow accents and mirrored surfaces, and features a padded stage and a small ball pool. It arranges a private and quiet space for reading, rest, or even impromptu play performances.

3. Suspension bridge and secret openings
The suspension bridge connects the cosplay theater with the play area and is structured with netted sides and secret hatches that lead to a giant ball pool and a transparent-top slide, expanding the dimensions of exploration for children as they climb and scale "walls," scoot down slides, and crawl through secret openings.

4. Galaxy sphere with UFO model
On the first floor, the galaxy sphere is completed with UFOs, a concrete floor, and a raised area that is painted a matching gray to provide a muted backdrop for art exhibitions. The UFO volumes sensationalize the space adventure experience with their dome structures that are fitted with padded interiors and lights to double as cozy reading nooks.

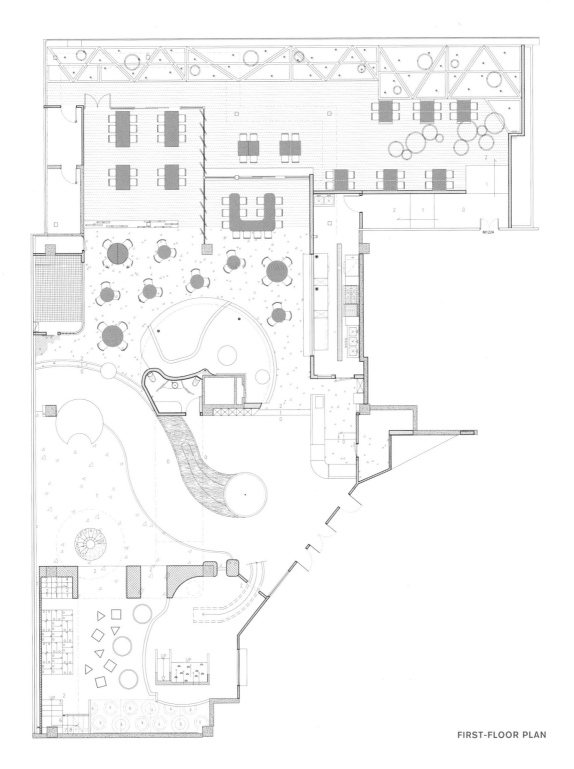

FIRST-FLOOR PLAN

Arc: Flexible, Ethereal, and Diverse

Antoni Gaudí once said that the line belongs to humans and the curve belongs to God. Arced elements are subtly blended into the design, striving for fluidity and separation of space. The curves build a relaxed and naturally inviting space that is attractive and appealing to children as a living space.

White Space: Personality Cultivating

In order to highlight the potential for subjective observations in children, a modern, simple style is employed. The main color palette of gray, matched with wood tones and bright French windows enlarges the activity space for children.

Light and Shadow: Inspiring Curiosity

The effects of light and shadow may be common details to adults, however, when contained within a small, dark space where it is the main focus, it takes on a new dimension of fascination, attracting children's attention, urging them on to explore the world.

Sculpture: Perceiving and Creating Beauty

The spatial forms of the dark space/lighthouse, semicircular cave theater, and bridge give the space a sculptural feel. Simple materials delicately conform, bend, and wrap to tailor a world of adventure that is visually impactful, and which narrates a story of beauty and art to children.

Preparing for an Adventure

By threading the experience of Space Art Home with stories of adventure, the center aims to forge close bonds between parents and children. By centering on family, the establishment promotes interaction and communication between parent and child within a context of exploration and "learning by experiencing."

Spatial Layout

Children are naturally curious about the unknown world. Hence, the space divides each activity zone into specific areas separate from the other, arranging the layout into play areas, an art exhibition area, workshop areas, and an outdoor animal field.

Such an arrangement helps create a dedicated world for children, where accompanying parents also get to have a taste of the children's unique fantasy world, in an aim to help parents connect with children on an equal level in order to form intimate bonds. In Star Art Home, fun and discovery are not the only goals. Parent-child relations and interactions are also considered, in order to create a truly unifying and holistic experience.

Dining Hall

Marked by bright French widows and the main color background of gray and white, with accents of color, the dining hall exudes a tasteful and comfortable ambiance. Warm wood tones, tactile finishes, and a simple and fresh design language come together to present a family-friendly and relaxed dining space.

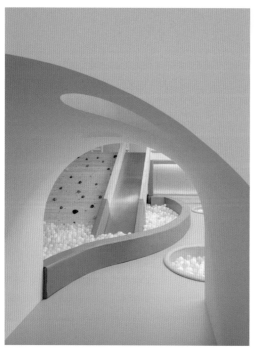

Play Area

The play area—featuring all-time favorites of children like ball pools, slides, a suspension bridge, trampoline, and building blocks—is integrated into the dining hall, so that children can have their fun and parents can relax and still keep an eye on them.

Art Exhibition Area

It is very important for children to have the ability to perceive and create beauty from an early age.

But far more important is the cultivation of children's aesthetic ability. The ability to appreciate beauty is just as, if not more important than the ability to create beauty, for how would a person who does not know how to appreciate beauty be able to create beautiful things?

The art exhibition space, therefore, aims to cultivate this appreciation of art and beauty, so children can one day create beautiful art of their own.

Central Kitchenette

All over the world, food and culture are often a united duo, usually going hand-in-hand. In that vein, the central kitchen hosts cooking workshops to expose children to recipes and different types of cooking methods to give them a taste of the world through cuisines from different parts of the globe.

The workshops also encourage children to try new things and develop their creativity, as well as help them cultivate patience, concentration, observation, thinking skills, and the ability to handle situations and respond to them accordingly. Parents who accompany their children to class get the opportunity to observe their children in the kitchen and guide them through the various tasks, thereby establishing strong parent-child relationships. Through this activity, children also learn some form of life skills.

Outdoor Pasture

Through the variety of plants grown in the pasture, children get to learn about different crop types and their growing/farming methods with real-life examples. They also gain an awareness of how food they consume makes its way to their plate from a raw ingredient. This organic experience and the observations they gather contribute to children feeling like they are a part of nature, and in turn helps them build respect for the environment.

Index

Published in Australia in 2022 by
The Images Publishing Group Pty Ltd
ABN 89 059 734 431

Offices
Melbourne
Waterman Business Centre
Suite 64, Level 2 UL40
1341 Dandenong Road, Chadstone,
Victoria 3148
Australia
Tel: +61 3 8564 8122

New York
6 West 18th Street 4B
New York, NY 10011
United States
Tel: +1 212 645 1111

Shanghai
6F, Building C, 838 Guangji Road
Hongkou District, Shanghai 200434
China
Tel: +86 021 31260822

books@imagespublishing.com
www.imagespublishing.com

Copyright © The Images Publishing Group Pty Ltd 2022
The Images Publishing Group Reference Number: 1651

All photography is attributed in the project pages unless otherwise noted.
Page 7: Alexander Angelovskyi (Svoya Studio, Hello BABY)

A catalogue record for this
book is available from the
National Library of Australia

Title: Contemporary Creative Spaces for Children
Author: Joey Ho (Introduction)
ISBN: 9781864709384

Printed by Toppan Excel (Dongguan) Printing CO,. LTD.